#1 Teacher Recommended!

Summer Bridge ACTIVITIES®

BRIDGING GRADES
3 to 4

Carson Dellosa Education
Greensboro, North Carolina

Caution: Exercise activities may require adult supervision. Before beginning any exercise activity, consult a physician. Written parental permission is suggested for those using this book in group situations. Children should always warm up prior to beginning any exercise activity and should stop immediately if they feel any discomfort during exercise.

Caution: Before beginning any food activity, ask parents' permission and inquire about the child's food allergies and religious or other food restrictions.

Caution: Nature activities may require adult supervision. Before beginning any nature activity, ask parents' permission and inquire about the child's plant and animal allergies. Remind the child not to touch plants or animals during the activity without adult supervision.

Caution: Before completing any balloon activity, ask parents' permission and inquire about possible latex allergies. Also, remember that uninflated or popped balloons may present a choking hazard.

The authors and publisher are not responsible or liable for any injury that may result from performing the exercises or activities in this book.

Summer Bridge®
An imprint of Carson Dellosa Education
PO Box 35665
Greensboro, NC 27425 USA

ISBN 978-1-4838-1583-1

21-071231151

Table of Contents

Making the Most of *Summer Bridge Activities*®

This book will help your child review third grade skills and preview fourth grade skills. Inside, find lots of resources that encourage your child to practice, learn, and grow while getting a head start on the new school year ahead.

Just 15 Minutes a Day

...is all it takes to stay sharp with learning activities for each weekday, all summer long!

Month-by-Month Organization

Three color-coded sections match the three months of summer vacation. Each month begins with a goal-setting and vocabulary-building activity. You'll also find an introduction to the section's fitness and character-building focus.

Daily Activities

Two pages of activities are provided for each weekday. They'll take about 15 minutes to complete. Activities cover math, reading comprehension, writing, grammar, and more.

Special Features

FITNESS FLASH: Quick exercises to develop strength, flexibility, and fitness

CHARACTER CHECK: Ideas for developing kindness, honesty, tolerance, and more

FACTOID: Fun trivia facts

Plenty of Bonus Features
...match your child's needs and interests!

Bonus Activities

Social studies activities explore places, maps, and more—a perfect complement to summer travel. Science experiments invite your child to interact with the world and build critical thinking skills.

Take It Outside!

A collection of fun ideas for outdoor observation, exploration, learning, and play is provided for each summer month.

Skill-Building Flash Cards

Cut out the cards at the back of the book. Store in a zip-top bag or punch a hole in each one and thread on a ring. Take the cards along with you for practice on the go.

Give a High-Five
...to your child for a job well done!

Star Stickers

Use the star stickers at the back of the book. Place a sticker in the space provided at the end of each day's learning activities when the pages are complete.

Praise and Rewards

After completing learning activities for a whole week or month, offer a reward. It could be a special treat, an outing, or time spent together. Praise the progress your child has made.

Certificate of Congratulations

At the end of the summer, complete and present the certificate at the back of the book. Congratulate your child for being well prepared for the next school year.

Skills Matrix

Day	Addition & Subtraction	Character Development	Fitness	Fractions	Geometry	Graphing & Probability	Language Arts & Writing	Measurement	Multiplication & Division	Numbers	Parts of Speech	Place Value	Prefixes & Suffixes	Problem Solving	Punctuation & Capitalization	Reading Comprehension	Science	Sentence Structure	Social Studies	Spelling	Vocabulary	Word Study
1														★		★					★	
2									★	★					★							★
3	★					★			★				★									
4						★	★				★			★								
5									★		★					★						
6			★						★		★			★								
7						★			★	★							★					
8								★							★							
9								★								★						
10				★	★						★								★			
11		★							★		★										★	
12									★				★									
13									★							★						★
14				★			★	★														
15				★							★			★							★	
16			★				★				★		★									
17									★							★						
18							★		★		★											
19							★		★							★						
20	★								★		★											
							★			★	BONUS PAGES!						★		★			
1							★		★							★						
2							★		★							★					★	
3			★						★				★							★		
4					★		★														★	
5	★				★			★			★											
6									★	★											★	
7	★						★		★									★				
8			★				★	★							★							
9							★									★				★		
10	★								★				★								★	
11	★						★					★									★	

vi

© Carson Dellosa Education

Skills Matrix

Day	Addition & Subtraction	Character Development	Fitness	Fractions	Geometry	Graphing & Probability	Language Arts & Writing	Measurement	Multiplication & Division	Numbers	Parts of Speech	Place Value	Prefixes & Suffixes	Problem Solving	Punctuation & Capitalization	Reading Comprehension	Science	Sentence Structure	Social Studies	Spelling	Vocabulary	Word Study
12					★							★			★	★						
13					★					★						★					★	
14				★		★	★				★											
15							★							★								
16		★					★								★	★						
17				★				★							★	★						
18				★					★												★	
19	★			★					★												★	★
20				★												★				★		
							★									BONUS PAGES!	★		★		★	
1	★						★		★							★				★		
2			★				★									★						
3							★									★						
4							★	★	★	★												
5			★	★								★				★						
6				★												★					★	
7				★			★	★								★						
8					★											★						★
9					★		★				★			★								
10				★			★									★						
11	★	★					★															
12							★		★							★						
13				★			★														★	★
14				★											★	★						
15									★							★		★				
16	★						★				★					★						
17	★			★												★		★				
18							★								★	★						
19					★		★									★						
20	★											★				★						
							★	★								BONUS PAGES!	★		★			

Summer Reading for Everyone

Reading is the single most important skill for school success. Experts recommend that third and fourth grade students read for at least 25 minutes each day. Help your child choose several books from this list based on his or her interests. Choose at least one fiction (F) and one nonfiction (NF) title. Then, head to the local library to begin your reading adventure!

If you like animals...
Two's a Crowd
   by Flora Ahn (F)
Ultimate Bugopedia
   by Darlyne Murawski
   and Nancy Honovich (NF)

If you like stories about inventions...
Rosie Revere, Engineer
   by Andrea Beaty (F)
Whoosh!: Lonnie Johnson's Super-Soaking Stream of Inventions
   by Chris Barton (NF)

If you like adventure stories...
The Wild Robot
   by Peter Brown (F)
Titanic: Voices from the Disaster
   by Deborah Hopkinson (NF)

If you like stories about the past...
I Survived the Eruption of Mount St. Helens, 1980
   by Lauren Tarshis (F)
The Tree Lady: The True Story of How One Tree-Loving Woman Changed a City Forever
   by Joseph Hopkins (NF)

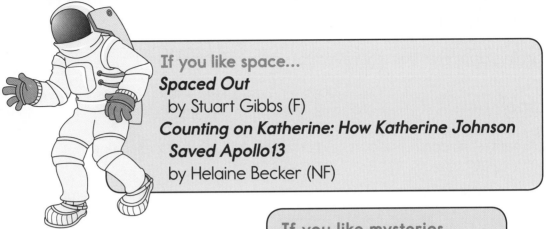

If you like space...
Spaced Out
  by Stuart Gibbs (F)
Counting on Katherine: How Katherine Johnson Saved Apollo13
  by Helaine Becker (NF)

If you like poetry...
Where the Sidewalk Ends
  by Shel Silverstein (F)
Horton Hatches the Egg
  by Dr. Seuss (F)

If you like mysteries...
Framed!
  by James Ponti (F)
History's Mysteries: Curious Clues, Cold Cases, and Puzzles from the Past
  by Kitson Jazynka (NF)

If you like comic books and graphic novels...
Giants Beware!
  by Jorge Aguirre (F)
Smile
  by Raina Telgemeier (NF)

If you like sports...
The Boy Who Saved Baseball
  by John Ritter (F)
Who Are Venus and Serena Williams?
  by James Buckley Jr. (NF)

If you like stories about the environment...
Ada's Violin: The Story of the Recycled Orchestra of Paraguay
  by Susan Hood and Sally Wern Comport (NF)
A River Ran Wild
  by Lynne Cherry (NF)

Summer Learning Is Everywhere!

Find learning opportunities wherever you go, all summer long!

Reading

- Experiment with reading indoors and outside in different places to find where you are most comfortable reading.

- Pick an interesting part of a book to read aloud to a friend or family member.

Language Arts

- Write a mysterious short story and see if a friend can guess the ending before they finish it.

- Write a poem to recite outdoors for friends or family members.

Math

- Make a math-based version of your favorite board game and play it with a friend.

- Practice estimating things like the number of items on a shelf using multiplication and division.

Science & Social Studies

- Learn about animal behavior for some of the nearby wildlife. Observe animals at a distance and keep track of what they do. Teach what you learned.

- Spend time with a grandparent or another older person. Teach them a game, song, or dance you like. Ask them to teach you a game, song, or dance from when they were your age.

Character & Fitness

- Make a list of three kind things to do that make your day better. Practice doing these things for others at least once a week.

- Learn how to use a new physical skill. It could be skipping rope, throwing a baseball, or even doing a new dance. Keep trying until you feel confident.

Monthly Goals

A goal is something that you want to accomplish. Sometimes, reaching a goal can be hard work!

Think of three goals to set for yourself this month. For example, you may want to read for 20 minutes each day. Write your goals on the lines and review them with an adult.

Place a sticker next to each of your goals that you complete. Feel proud that you have met your goals!

1. _____

PLACE STICKER HERE

2. _____

PLACE STICKER HERE

3. _____

PLACE STICKER HERE

Word List

The following words are used in this section. They are good words for you to know. Read each word. Use a dictionary to look up each word that you do not know. Then, write two sentences. Use a word from the word list in each sentence.

briefly	exhibition
bronze	glacier
concentrate	league
design	relief
displayed	representing

1. _____

   _____

2. _____

   _____

Introduction to Flexibility

This section includes fitness and character development activities that focus on flexibility. These activities are designed to get you moving and thinking about building your physical fitness and your character. If you have limited mobility, feel free to modify any suggested exercises to fit your individual abilities.

Physical Flexibility

For many people, being flexible means easily doing everyday tasks, such as bending to tie a shoe. Tasks like this can be hard for people who do not stretch often.

Stretching will make your muscles more flexible. It can also improve your balance and coordination.

You probably stretch every day without realizing it. Do you ever reach for a dropped pencil or a box of cereal on the top shelf? If you do, then you are stretching. Try to improve your flexibility this summer. Set a stretching goal. For example, you might stretch every day until you can touch your toes.

Flexibility of Character

It is good to have a flexible body. It is also good to be mentally flexible. This means being open to change.

It can be upsetting when things do not go your way. Can you think of a time when an unexpected event ruined your plans? For example, a trip to the zoo was canceled because the car had a flat tire. Unexpected events happen sometimes. How you react to those events often affects the outcome. Arm yourself with the tools to be flexible. Have realistic expectations. Find ways to make bad situations better. Look for good things that may come from disappointing events.

You can be mentally flexible by showing respect to other people. Sharing and accepting the differences of other people are also ways to be mentally flexible. This character trait gets easier with practice. Over the summer, practice and use your mental flexibility often.

Solve each word problem.

1. Don is picking apples. He puts 36 apples in each box. How many apples does he put in 9 boxes?

2. Miss Brown has 25 students in her class. She wants to make 5 equal teams for a relay race. How many students will be on each team?

3. Zack has saved $9.00 toward buying a new ball. He will get $3.00 today from his father. How much more money will he need to buy the $19.95 ball?

4. Jenna saves 867 pennies in May, 942 in June, and 716 in July. How much does she save in these three months?

Read each group of related words. Write two more related words for each group.
EXAMPLE:

		quail	pheasant
	robin, owl, pigeon		
5.	peaches, apples, pears		
6.	spoon, bowl, cup		
7.	lake, pond, river		
8.	branches, sticks, wood		
9.	lemonade, water, milk		
10.	dollar, dime, penny		
11.	carrot, celery, cucumber		
12.	dress, shoes, skirt		
13.	tennis, golf, racquetball		

Read the passage. Then, answer the questions.

Glaciers

A glacier is a large, thick mass of ice. It forms when snow hardens into ice over a long period of time. It might not look like it, but glaciers can move. Glaciers usually move slowly. If a lot of ice melts at once, a glacier may **surge** forward, or move suddenly. Most glaciers are found in Antarctica (the continent at the South Pole) or in Greenland (a country near the North Pole). Areas with glaciers receive a lot of snowfall in the winter and have cool summers. Most glaciers are located in the mountains where few people live. Occasionally, glaciers can cause flooding in cities and towns. Falling ice from glaciers may block the path of people hiking on trails farther down the mountain. Icebergs are large, floating pieces of ice that have broken off from glaciers. Icebergs can cause problems for ships at sea.

14. What is the main idea of this passage?
    A. Icebergs can be dangerous to ships.
    B. Glaciers are large masses of ice found mainly in the mountains.
    C. People usually live far away from glaciers.

15. How does a glacier form? _____

    _____

16. What does the word *surge* mean in this passage?
    A. move forward suddenly
    B. freeze into ice
    C. break off from an iceberg

17. Where are most glaciers located? _____

18. What is the weather like where glaciers are found? _____

19. What effects can glaciers have on humans?_____

    _____

FACTOID: Glaciers store about 75% of Earth's freshwater.

PLACE STICKER HERE

Write the base word of each word.

1. playful _____

2. disinterest _____

3. rewrite _____

4. uncover _____

5. spoonful _____

6. quickly _____

7. happiness _____

8. doubtful _____

9. kindness _____

10. recover _____

Follow the directions.

11. Draw a square around the greatest number.

12. Count by twos to 40. Underline the numbers you use.

13. Draw a triangle around the number that is 4 less than 62.

14. Draw an X over each odd number.

15. Circle all of the uppercase letters. Write the letters you circled in order, starting with the top row and moving left to right.

_____

b	r	q	e	o	S	c	r	y	10	6	3
U	y	10	5	2	4	M	z	1	q	a	i
6	v	0	7	8	M	p	2	10	17	12	l
r	b	14	18	b	e	16	f	h	19	E	s
18	5	14	7	2	p	m	n	z	58	20	s
94	86	22	2	R	17	I	0	24	n	x	c
26	39	3	a	d	e	28	g	S	52	19	30
7	j	F	k	32	y	34	4	31	t	10	36
0	n	e	n	38	o	80	98	U	47	x	p
w	m	m	11	N	3	14	39	c	r	e	t
q	u	v	9	7	6	w	5	40	w	13	19

CHARACTER CHECK: Look up the word *considerate* in a dictionary. Then, think of two ways that you can be considerate.

DAY 2

Use the fact family in each circle to make number sentences.

16.

$$\begin{array}{c} 3 \\ 6 \quad 18 \end{array}$$

_____ × _____ = _____

_____ × _____ = _____

_____ ÷ _____ = _____

_____ ÷ _____ = _____

17.

$$\begin{array}{c} 9 \\ 4 \quad 36 \end{array}$$

_____ × _____ = _____

_____ × _____ = _____

_____ ÷ _____ = _____

_____ ÷ _____ = _____

18.

$$\begin{array}{c} 6 \\ 8 \quad 48 \end{array}$$

_____ × _____ = _____

_____ × _____ = _____

_____ ÷ _____ = _____

_____ ÷ _____ = _____

Each important word in a title should begin with a capital letter. Read the sentences. Draw three short lines under each letter that should be a capital, like this: c̲.

19. On the way to vacation, we listened to the audiobook *How to eat fried worms*.

20. Mom gets a little teary when she hears the Beatles song "let it Be."

21. This year, the high school is putting on the musical "My fair Lady."

22. If you like mysteries, read *Watcher in the piney woods*.

23. At Ruby's sleepover, we watched *how to train your dragon*.

24. Cameron memorized Robert Frost's poem "Stopping by woods on a snowy evening."

25. At camp this summer, I learned the song "On Top of spaghetti."

26. My sister and I have watched the movie *frozen* four times.

FITNESS FLASH: Touch your toes 10 times.

* See page ii.

PLACE STICKER HERE

Add to find each sum.

1.	634 + 68	2.	87 +89	3.	493 + 77	4.	888 + 45	5.	732 + 99

6.	47 +76	7.	496 + 94	8.	557 + 23	9.	347 + 54	10.	665 + 37

Rewrite each set of underlined words to make it a possessive.

11. Have you seen <u>the mitten belonging to Margot</u>? _____

12. The <u>towels belonging to the boys</u> are in the dryer. _____

13. We put <u>the bike belonging to Salim</u> in the garage. _____

14. The <u>chirping of the birds</u> woke me up. _____

15. <u>The hat belonging to Charles</u> is navy and red. _____

16. "The <u>leaves of the maple tree</u> have begun to fall!" said Jax. _____

17. <u>The books belonging to Kylie</u> are on the counter. _____

18. Lauren lost <u>the goggles belonging to Mariko</u> in the pool. _____

FACTOID: There are more than 10,000 known species of ants on Earth.

DAY 3

Read the story. Then, write the correct prefix in each blank. Use *dis-*, *in-*, *re-*, or *un-*.

My Uncle Paul worked in a bookstore. Uncle Paul always helped me find books to read.

He was never (19.) _____ pleased if I asked him for help. I (20.) _____ call

the day I asked for a book about unsolved mysteries. Uncle Paul

(21.) _____ covered some on the very top of the back shelf. They were dirty and

smelled dusty. They looked as if they had been (22.) _____ touched for years.

I started to read one. As I looked (23.) _____ side, I noticed that some of the

pages were missing from the very end of the book. "Oh no!" I said. "This story is

(24.) _____ complete. Now, I'll never know how it ends." I must have looked pretty

(25.) _____ appointed because Uncle Paul tried to cheer me up. He said, "I think you

(26.) _____ covered a real unsolved mystery!"

Choose three words with prefixes from the story. Write the words and their meanings on the lines.

_____

_____

_____

Solve the problems.

27. 30
    × 9

28. 50
    × 5

29. 80
    × 3

30. 90
    × 7

31. 40
    × 6

32. 20
    × 8

8

PLACE
STICKER
HERE

Solve each word problem.

1. I read 6 books each month in June, July, and August. How many books did I read during these three months?

2. Carla went on a trip. She took 120 photos during her 3-day trip. How many photos did she take each day?

3. Josie observed birds in her backyard for one week. She saw 6 birds each day. How many birds did she see in all?

4. Nico had a sleepover and invited 7 friends. His stepmom made 32 mini muffins for breakfast. How many muffins could each boy have?

Underline the word that correctly completes each sentence.

5. Luis and Kate (is, are) looking for something to do on a sunny day.

6. They decide to (makes, make) an obstacle course.

7. Kate drags out a few old tires that (her, she) dad said were in the garage.

8. Luis (brings, bring) over three pool noodles.

9. "What else can (us, we) use?" wonders Kate aloud.

10. "I (see, sees) a few big branches that might work," suggests Luis.

11. After a lot of work, Kate and Luis are satisfied with (our, their) obstacle course.

12. "Who should (try, tries) it first?" asks Kate.

DAY 4

Study the pictograph. Then, answer each question.

Month	Tires Sold
Jan.	⭕⭕⭕⭕⭕◖
Feb.	⭕⭕
March	⭕◖
April	⭕⭕⭕◖
May	⭕

Key
⭕ = 500 tires

13. How many more tires were sold in April than in February?

_____

14. What is the difference between the least number of tires sold in a month and the greatest number of tires sold in a month?

_____

An *adjective* is a word that describes a noun. Circle the adjective that describes each underlined noun.

15. Some prairie dogs live in large <u>communities</u> under the ground.

16. A mother prairie dog makes a nest of dried <u>plants</u> in the spring.

17. She gives birth to a litter of four <u>pups</u>.

18. She is a good <u>mother</u> and takes care of her pups.

19. The pups are ready to venture outside after six <u>weeks</u>.

20. The pups have many <u>friends</u>.

FITNESS FLASH: Do 10 shoulder shrugs.

* See page ii.

PLACE STICKER HERE

Read the passage. Then, answer the questions.

The Olympic Games

During the Olympic Games, people from all over the world gather to compete in different sporting events. The original Olympics were held in Greece around 776 B.C. Athletes came together every four years to run races of different lengths. Those who won were given wreaths of olive branches. The modern Olympics were first held in 1896 in Greece. In 1994, the International Olympic Committee decided that the summer and winter Olympic Games should be held in different years. This means that every two years, thousands of people **representing** more than 200 countries come together to compete in either summer or winter sports. Today's top athletes receive gold, silver, or bronze medals and compete in hundreds of different events. The Olympics give each host country a chance to show its culture both to the people who come there and to the people who watch on TV. The sports may be different than in the original Olympics, but the spirit of goodwill and good sportsmanship is still the same.

1. What is the main idea of this passage?
    A. The Olympics are held every four years.
    B. People come to the Olympics from all over the world to compete in different sports.
    C. Today's top athletes receive gold, silver, or bronze medals.

2. When and where were the original Olympics held? _____

3. What did winners receive at the early Olympics? _____

4. How did the Olympics change in 1994? _____

    _____

5. What does the word *representing* mean? _____

    _____

6. How do the Olympics help people learn about different cultures? _____

    _____

DAY 5

Find the value of *?* in each problem below.

7.   6 × (5 × ?) = (6 × 5) × 12   ? = _____

8.   (? × 9) × 3 = 16 × (9 × 3)   ? = _____

9.   (5 × 8) × 10 = 5 × (? × 10)   ? = _____

10.   2 × (? × 6) = (2 × 14) × 6   ? = _____

11.   (? × 6) × 11 = 9 × (6 × 11)   ? = _____

12.   5 × (5 × ?) = (5 × 5) × 8   ? = _____

13.   (14 × ?) × 6 = 14 × (3 × 6)   ? = _____

14.   20 × (4 × 7) = (? × 4) × 7   ? = _____

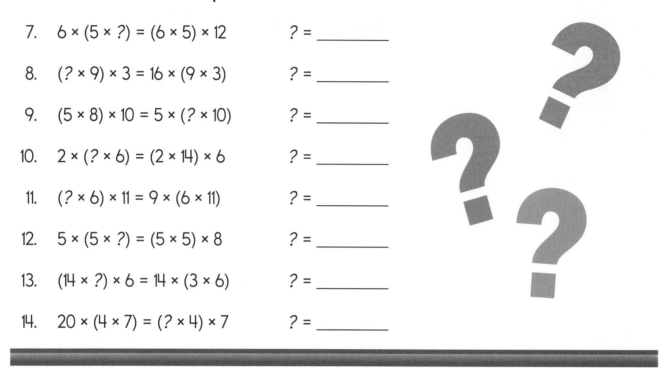

Write the correct forms of each adjective.

	Adjectives That Compare Two Nouns	Adjectives That Compare More Than Two Nouns
EXAMPLE:		
long	longer	longest
15. soft		
16. large		
17. flat		
18. sweet		
19. wide		
20. cool		

PLACE STICKER HERE

Solve each problem.

1. 25 ÷ 5 = _____

2. 4 × 16 = _____

3. 81 ÷ 9 = _____

4. 28 ÷ 4 = _____

5. 36 ÷ 6 = _____

6. 9 × 2 = _____

7. 11 × 9 = _____

8. 14 × 6 = _____

9. 39 ÷ 3 = _____

10. 6 × 11 = _____

11. 18 ÷ 3 = _____

12. 10 × 3 = _____

13. 14 ÷ 7 = _____

14. 5 × 6 = _____

15. 7 × 7 = _____

The Athletic Advantage

There are a lot of benefits to stretching. Do you like basketball, dancing, or another physical activity that requires you to move, run, or jump? If so, then you should try to improve your flexibility. Whatever your favorite physical activity is, set a goal for yourself to complete at least one stretch every day that will help make you a better athlete. For example, if you like tennis and want to improve your backhand, practice a trunk-twist stretch at least twice a day. As with all stretching exercises, start slowly. Gradually increase your stretching as you become more flexible. This is how professional athletes improve their abilities. So, stretch for better performance!

* See page ii.

DAY 6

Solve each word problem. Show your work.

16. Bobbi made 8 quarts of punch for the party. How many cups did she make?	17. Together, two boxes of spices weigh 4 pounds 8 ounces. Each pound is worth $400. How much are the boxes worth in all?
18. Ms. Lackey gave each student in her class a calculator. Each calculator weighed 16 ounces. If Ms. Lackey gave each of her 20 students a calculator, how many pounds did the calculators weigh in all?	19. Virginia's school ordered 20 boxes of milk. In each box, there were 35 containers of milk. By the end of the week, 265 containers were used. How many containers were left?

A *noun* names a person, a place, or a thing. An *action verb* tells what a noun is doing. Circle the nouns. Underline the verbs.

elephant	sang	ate	fixed
laugh	tent	Mr. Chip	team
book	California	guitar	landed
Lake Street	cleaned	yell	played
visited	Kent	write	strength
engine	see	broccoli	tasted

FACTOID: Saturn is the only planet in our solar system that could float on water.

PLACE STICKER HERE

Abstract nouns are feelings, concepts, and ideas. Some examples are *hope*, *bravery*, and *pride*. Underline the abstract noun in each sentence.

1. Colonel Graham knows that the cadets respect him.

2. We were so grateful for our neighbors' generosity after the fire.

3. "I am almost out of patience," warned Mom.

4. We could see Izzy's satisfaction when she finally finished the puzzle.

5. Ryan's silliness made the whole group laugh.

6. Dionne showed courage when he faced the auditorium and started to speak.

Study the bar graph. Then, answer each question.

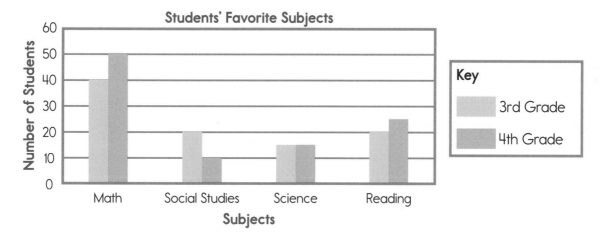

7. What is the total number of students who like social studies?

_____

8. How many total students are in 3rd grade? Fourth grade?

_____

9. Which subjects have the greatest difference between 3rd and 4th grade?

_____

10. How many more students like math than reading in 3rd grade? Fourth grade?

_____

DAY 7

Round each number to the nearest 10.

EXAMPLE:

28 = __30__   11.   85 = _____   12.   13 = _____   13.   44 = _____

14.   33 = _____   15.   92 = _____   16.   78 = _____   17.   18 = _____

Round each number to the nearest 100.

18.   767 = _____   19.   841 = _____   20.   211 = _____   21.   587 = _____

Read each sentence. On the line, write *S* if it is a simple sentence, *C* if it is a compound sentence, and *CX* if it is a complex sentence. Then, underline each conjunction in the compound and complex sentences.

22.   _____   Before school starts, Jada wants a new backpack.

23.   _____   Mr. O'Rourke retired from teaching last year.

24.   _____   Unless you finish your homework, we won't be able to watch the movie.

25.   _____   Owen and Rosie are going camping today, but they'll be back on Sunday.

26.   _____   We can cook chicken, or we can go out for dinner.

27.   _____   Although I like to ride my bike, I'm going to roller-skate to Jenna's house today.

28.   _____   Nazim is going to vacuum, and Molly is going to dust.

29.   _____   Because Gabriela lost the book, she'll have to pay a fine.

FITNESS FLASH: Practice a V-sit. Stretch five times.

* See page ii.

PLACE STICKER HERE

Jonah and his mom are building a raised garden bed for the backyard. Jonah measures the boards he finds in the shed that might be useful. Draw an X above the line plot to show the length of each board.

$42\frac{1}{2}$ inches	$46\frac{3}{4}$ inches
42 inches	$40\frac{1}{4}$ inches
$46\frac{3}{4}$ inches	$42\frac{1}{2}$ inches
$40\frac{1}{4}$ inches	$40\frac{1}{4}$ inches
$42\frac{1}{2}$ inches	$40\frac{1}{4}$ inches
$46\frac{3}{4}$ inches	44 inches

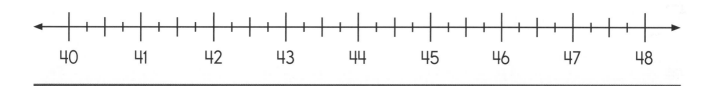

40   41   42   43   44   45   46   47   48

To add commas where they are needed in the dialogue below, use a mark like this: ⌄ .

1. "I'd like to ride the Ferris wheel first" said Anya.

2. "I'll meet you over there" said Kahlil "after I get something to drink."

3. "The fair seems even more crowded this year than last" commented Riley.

4. "My favorite attraction is the bumper cars" said Jacob "but I also love the giant slides."

5. "I can't go on anything that spins" said Kahlil "because it makes me feel sick."

6. Riley pointed and said "There's the frozen lemonade stand."

7. Anya asked "What time are you meeting your parents?"

8. "The line is too long for the rocket ship ride" decided Oliver.

DAY 8

Find the area of each figure.

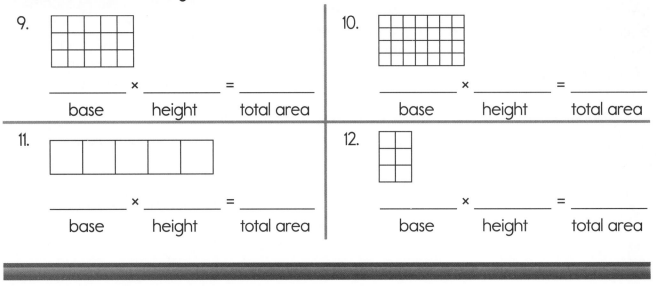

9.

_____ × _____ = _____
base   height   total area

10.

_____ × _____ = _____
base   height   total area

11.

_____ × _____ = _____
base   height   total area

12.

_____ × _____ = _____
base   height   total area

Estimate the volume or mass of each item. Circle your answer.

13. one peanut

A. 1 gram   B. 100 grams   C. 1 kilogram

14. the amount of liquid in one teaspoon

A. 5 milliliters   B. 50 milliliters   C. 500 milliliters

15. the amount of liquid a bathtub can hold

A. 1 liter   B. 150 liters   C. 15 milliliters

Solve each word problem. Hint: It might help to make drawings on a separate sheet of paper.

16. One apple weighs about 85 grams. How much would 4 apples weigh? _____

17. The DeMarco family is moving. Their largest box weighs 50 kilograms. It has a mass 5 times greater than the mass of their smallest box. What is the mass of their smallest box? _____

18. Jordan is using three containers for his experiment. One holds 150 milliliters, one holds 300 milliliters, and one holds 475 milliliters. How much do the containers hold in all? _____

PLACE
STICKER
HERE

Write the perimeter of each figure or the missing side lengths.

1.

35 yd.
35 yd.   35 yd.
35 yd.

perimeter = _____ yd.

2.

2 in.   2 in.
2 in.   2 in.
2 in.

perimeter = _____ in.

3.

8 cm   8 cm
4 cm

perimeter = _____ cm

4.

12 in.   18 in.
13 in.

perimeter = _____ in.

5.

50 mm
A   B
25 mm

perimeter = 235 mm

Side A = _____ mm   Side B = _____ mm

6.

A
5 cm   5 cm
5 cm   5 cm
5 cm   5 cm
B

perimeter = 40 cm

Side A = _____ cm   Side B = _____ cm

Solve the problems.

7. Mia's parents said that she can use a space in the yard that measures 13 feet long by 9 feet wide for her wildflower garden. What is the area of the garden?

8. Mr. Wen needs to replace a section of fence that measures 3 feet by 17 feet. What is the area of the fence that needs to be replaced?

9. Alysha wants to frame a drawing she made. It measures 8 inches by 12 inches. What is the area of the frame she needs?

10. Grandma Hattie made a baby quilt for Connor. It measures 4 feet by 3 feet. What is the area of the quilt?

DAY 9

Read the passage. Then, answer the questions.

Harriet Tubman

Harriet Tubman was a brave woman. She grew up as a slave in Maryland. As an adult, she escaped north to Pennsylvania. Tubman returned to Maryland to help rescue her family. She returned many times to help other slaves. She guided slaves to safety along a network known as the Underground Railroad. People who helped slaves move to freedom were called "conductors." They were named after the people who controlled trains on railroads. In 1861, the United States began fighting the Civil War. This war was a struggle between northern and southern states, partly over whether people should be allowed to own slaves. President Abraham Lincoln signed a law in 1863. The law stated that slavery was no longer allowed in the United States. With the law on her side, Tubman continued for many years to help people who were treated unfairly.

11. What is the main idea of this passage?
    A. "Conductors" were people who helped slaves move to freedom.
    B. Harriet Tubman lived in Maryland.
    C. Harriet Tubman helped people on the Underground Railroad.

12. Why did Tubman return to Maryland? _____

    _____

13. What was the Underground Railroad? _____

    _____

14. What did conductors on the Underground Railroad do? _____

    _____

15. What was the Civil War? _____

    _____

FITNESS FLASH: Do arm circles for 30 seconds.

* See page ii.

PLACE
STICKER
HERE

Draw a line between fractions that are equivalent, or equal.

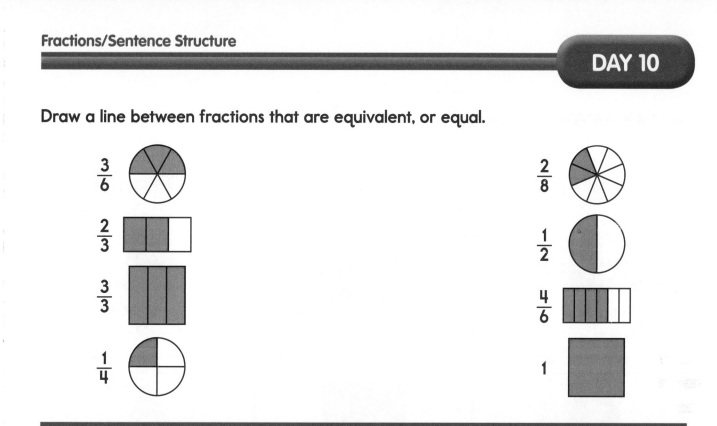

$\dfrac{3}{6}$

$\dfrac{2}{3}$

$\dfrac{3}{3}$

$\dfrac{1}{4}$

$\dfrac{2}{8}$

$\dfrac{1}{2}$

$\dfrac{4}{6}$

1

Combine each pair of simple sentences to write compound sentences. Use the conjunction shown in parentheses ( ). Do not forget to write a comma before the conjunction in each sentence.

EXAMPLE:

We might go to the park. We might go to the store. (or)

We might go to the park, or we might go to the store.

1. My dog is ready to play. My cat wants to nap. (but)

   _____

   _____

2. It may rain tonight. The party will be indoors. (so)

   _____

   _____

DAY 10

Label each shape with letters from the box that describe it.

A = quadrilateral	B = parallelogram	C = rhombus	D = polygon

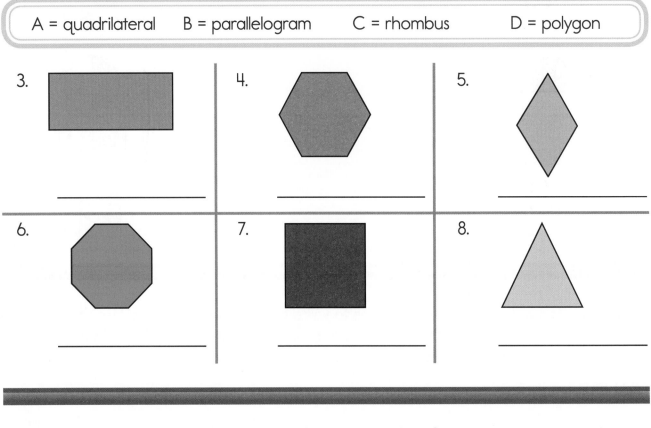

3. _____

4. _____

5. _____

6. _____

7. _____

8. _____

A *possessive pronoun* is a pronoun that shows ownership. Some possessive pronouns include:

mine	ours	your	his	hers	their	its	my	our

Write five sentences. Use a possessive pronoun in each sentence.

9. _____

10. _____

11. _____

12. _____

13. _____

PLACE STICKER HERE

Write the word from the word bank that matches each description.

knead	sense	praise	certain
wheat	purchase	numb	guide

1. unable to feel   _____

2. we do this to dough   _____

3. sure of something   _____

4. to buy something   _____

5. to see, hear, feel, taste, or smell   _____

6. flour is made from this   _____

7. a leader of a group   _____

8. to express approval   _____

Compassion Collage

Compassion is seeing that someone needs help or understanding and offering him support. Create a compassion collage. Think about ways that people show compassion. Cut out compassion pictures and words from magazines and newspapers. Use markers, poster board, and glue to create your collage. Draw small pictures, write words, and add stickers to the collage. Give your collage a title, such as *The Cs of Compassion: Care, Concern, Consider.* Display the collage so that others can see how you have captured compassion.

DAY 11

Divide to find each quotient.

9. 3)18   10. 4)24   11. 3)21   12. 4)36   13. 8)32

14. 5)40   15. 6)36   16. 9)36   17. 8)40   18. 9)27

Write an adjective in each blank to complete each sentence.

19. A _____ family moved in next door yesterday.

20. The bear has _____ , _____ fur.

21. The _____ birds woke me up this morning.

22. Her _____ , _____ balloon floated away.

Demonstrative adjectives identify specific people, places, or things. Write the correct demonstrative adjective (*this, that, these,* or *those*) to complete each sentence. Use *this* and *that* with singular nouns. Use *these* and *those* with plural nouns.

23. _____ book is one of my favorites.

24. Is _____ hat the one Mom wanted?

25. _____ planet is very far away.

26. _____ ducks didn't come back to the pond this year.

FACTOID: Rain has never been recorded at the center of Chile's Atacama Desert.

PLACE STICKER HERE

Divide each set of objects into the correct number of groups.

EXAMPLE:

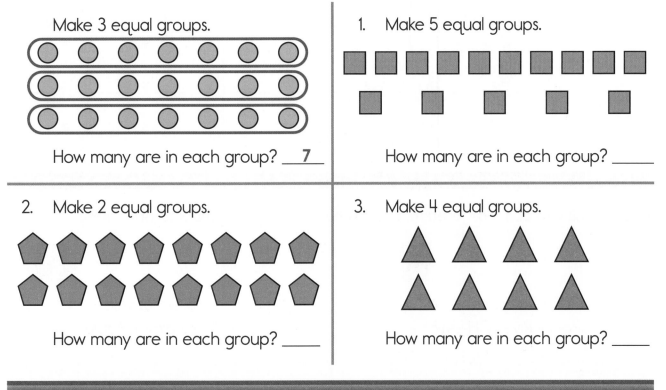

Make 3 equal groups.

How many are in each group? __7__

1. Make 5 equal groups.

How many are in each group? _____

2. Make 2 equal groups.

How many are in each group? _____

3. Make 4 equal groups.

How many are in each group? _____

Add commas where they belong in each sentence.

EXAMPLE:

August 10, 1970, and May 10, 1973, are birth dates in our family.

4. My mom and stepdad were married in Portland Oregon on May 1 1999.

5. We had chicken potatoes corn gravy and ice cream for dinner.

6. George Washington became the first U.S. president on April 30 1789.

7. Sam was born on June 16 1947 in Rome Italy.

8. We saw deer bears elk and goats on our trip.

9. On July 24 1962 in Boise Idaho I won the big race.

DAY 12

Complete each fact family.

10. 5 × 3 = _____

_____ × _____ = _____

_____ ÷ _____ = _____

_____ ÷ _____ = _____

11. 21 ÷ 3 = _____

_____ ÷ _____ = _____

_____ × _____ = _____

_____ × _____ = _____

12. 30 ÷ 6 = _____

_____ ÷ _____ = _____

_____ × _____ = _____

_____ × _____ = _____

Add the missing commas to each address below. Use this symbol to add them: ⌄.

13.
19052 Tanglewood Dr.
Rocky River OH 44116

16.
133 Greenvale Rd.
Lincoln NE 68516

14.
958 East Oak Lane #17
Baltimore MD 21218

17.
21896 Sardis Court
Portland OR 97215

15.
35 Frog Creek Woods
Harrisburg PA 17111

18.
568 Elm Street
Colton CA 92324

FITNESS FLASH: Practice a V-sit. Stretch five times.

* See page ii.

PLACE STICKER HERE

Use the distributive property to make the problems easier to solve.

EXAMPLE: 8 × 16 =
$(8 × 10) + (8 × 6) = 128$

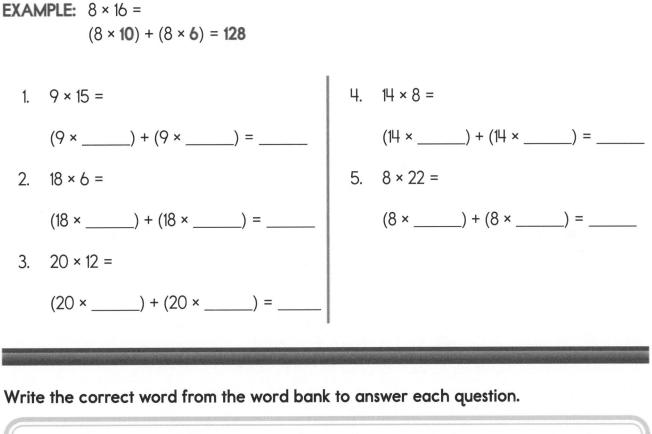

1.   9 × 15 =

   (9 × _____) + (9 × _____) = _____

2.   18 × 6 =

   (18 × _____) + (18 × _____) = _____

3.   20 × 12 =

   (20 × _____) + (20 × _____) = _____

4.   14 × 8 =

   (14 × _____) + (14 × _____) = _____

5.   8 × 22 =

   (8 × _____) + (8 × _____) = _____

Write the correct word from the word bank to answer each question.

night	different	hopped	baby	knock

6.   Which word begins with a silent letter?_____

7.   Which word has the *t* sound at the end, but the letter *t* is not making the sound?

   _____

8.   Which word has a silent *gh*? _____

9.   Which word has the long *e* sound but does not include the letter *e*?

   _____

10.   Which word has three syllables?_____

DAY 13

Read the passage. Then, answer the questions.

Roberto Clemente

Roberto Clemente was born in Puerto Rico in 1934. He played baseball in his neighborhood as a child. Then, he played for his high school team. He joined a junior national league when he was 16. He played baseball briefly in Canada before signing to play for the Pittsburgh Pirates in 1954. Clemente served in the U.S. Marine Reserves for several years. That helped him grow stronger physically. He helped the Pirates win two World Series. During the off-season, Clemente often went back to Puerto Rico to help people. He liked visiting children in hospitals to give them hope that they could get well. An earthquake hit the country of Nicaragua in 1972. At age 38, Clemente died in an airplane crash on his way to deliver supplies to Nicaragua. He was elected to the Baseball Hall of Fame in 1973. He was the first Latino player to receive that honor.

11. What is the main idea of this passage?
    A. Roberto Clemente was a great baseball player who also helped people.
    B. Roberto Clemente died in an airplane crash.
    C. Roberto Clemente was elected to the Baseball Hall of Fame.

12. Where was Clemente born? _____

13. Where in the United States did Clemente play baseball?_____

14. What did Clemente do during the off-season? _____

15. What happened in Nicaragua in 1972? _____

    _____

16. Why was Clemente flying to Nicaragua? _____

    _____

FACTOID: The rules of modern baseball were originally called the *Knickerbocker Rules*.

PLACE
STICKER
HERE

Compare the fractions. Use the greater than (>), less than (<), or equal to (=) symbols.

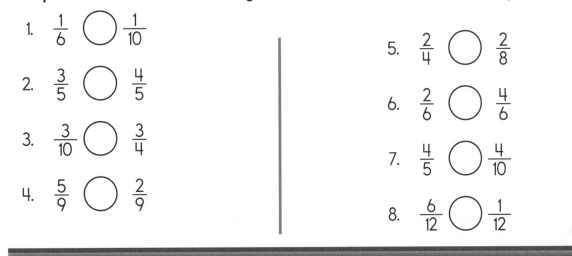

1. $\frac{1}{6}$ ◯ $\frac{1}{10}$

2. $\frac{3}{5}$ ◯ $\frac{4}{5}$

3. $\frac{3}{10}$ ◯ $\frac{3}{4}$

4. $\frac{5}{9}$ ◯ $\frac{2}{9}$

5. $\frac{2}{4}$ ◯ $\frac{2}{8}$

6. $\frac{2}{6}$ ◯ $\frac{4}{6}$

7. $\frac{4}{5}$ ◯ $\frac{4}{10}$

8. $\frac{6}{12}$ ◯ $\frac{1}{12}$

An *idiom* is a word or phrase that cannot be taken literally. Read each sentence below. Then, write the meaning of the underlined idiom.

9. Before Kayla went onstage last night, her parents gave her a kiss and told her to break a leg.

_____

10. Jorge is feeling under the weather, so he's going to stay home from school.

_____

11. Will and Myles are both going to a new camp this summer, so they are planning to stick together.

_____

12. Grandpa has a wonderful vegetable garden — he has quite a green thumb!

_____

13. Mom said that a new transmission for the car will cost an arm and a leg.

_____

DAY 14

Draw lines to divide each shape according to the fraction given.

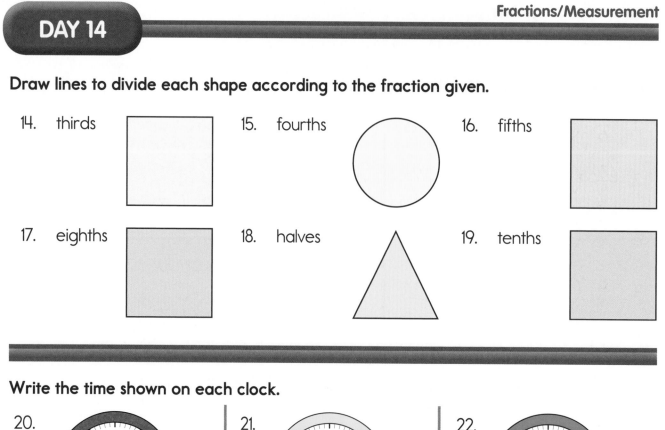

14. thirds

15. fourths

16. fifths

17. eighths

18. halves

19. tenths

Write the time shown on each clock.

20.

____ : ____

21.

____ : ____

22.

____ : ____

23.

____ : ____

24.

____ : ____

25.

____ : ____

FITNESS FLASH: Touch your toes 10 times.

* See page ii.

30

PLACE
STICKER
HERE

Solve each word problem. Show your work.

1. Today's high was 86°. Yesterday, it was 9° colder. Two days ago, it was 6° colder than yesterday. What was the high temperature two days ago?

2. Annabel is 53 inches tall. Nicholas is 4 feet 4 inches tall. How many inches taller is Annabel?

3. Terrell brought 42 muffins to school for his birthday. He gave one each to the 17 students in his class and to the 19 students in the other third-grade class. How many extra muffins did he have?

4. Natasha can ride her bike at a rate of 10 miles per hour. How many miles can she go if she rides from 10:00 A.M. to 3:00 P.M.?

Circle the word that does not belong in each group of words. Then, describe why the other words belong together.

5. tuba, clarinet, jazz, flute, harp _____

6. tire, hammer, screwdriver, wrench _____

7. robin, hawk, sparrow, dog, crow _____

8. Moon, Mars, Earth, Jupiter, Venus _____

9. lettuce, peach, carrot, peas, beets _____

10. rose, daisy, lazy, tulip, lily _____

DAY 15

Mark each fraction on the number line.

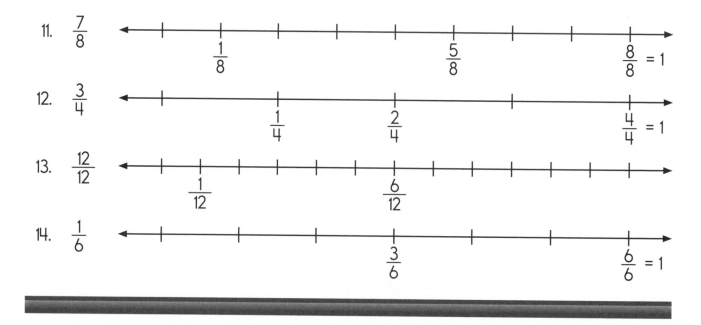

11. $\frac{7}{8}$ $\frac{1}{8}$ $\frac{5}{8}$ $\frac{8}{8} = 1$

12. $\frac{3}{4}$ $\frac{1}{4}$ $\frac{2}{4}$ $\frac{4}{4} = 1$

13. $\frac{12}{12}$ $\frac{1}{12}$ $\frac{6}{12}$

14. $\frac{1}{6}$ $\frac{3}{6}$ $\frac{6}{6} = 1$

Complete each sentence with the future-tense form of the verb in parentheses.

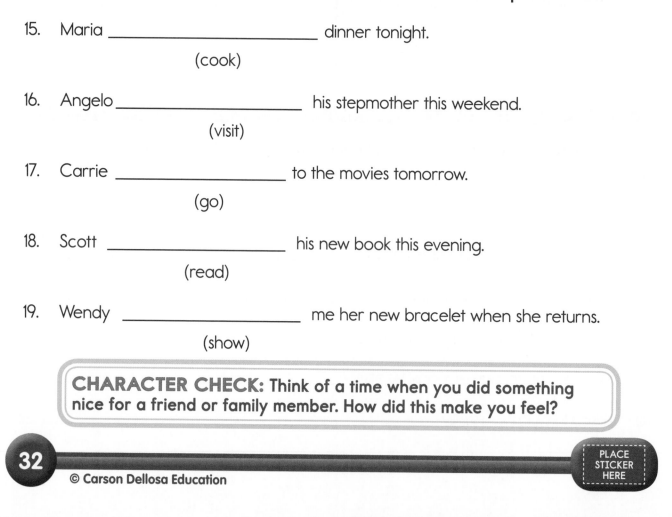

15. Maria _____ dinner tonight.
     (cook)

16. Angelo _____ his stepmother this weekend.
     (visit)

17. Carrie _____ to the movies tomorrow.
     (go)

18. Scott _____ his new book this evening.
     (read)

19. Wendy _____ me her new bracelet when she returns.
     (show)

CHARACTER CHECK: Think of a time when you did something nice for a friend or family member. How did this make you feel?

PLACE
STICKER
HERE

Add a suffix to each word. Use *-est*, *-tion*, or *-ty*. Double, drop, or change some letters if needed. Then, write the meaning of the new word.

EXAMPLE:

tasty _____**tastiest, most tasty**_____

1. sad _____

2. act_____

3. direct _____

4. safe _____

5. dirt_____

6. hungry _____

7. invent _____

8. prepare _____

9. happy_____

10. heavy_____

11. honest _____

Circle the pronouns in each sentence.

12. I told her about Janelle's horse.

13. This piece of cake is for him.

14. Liz invited Garrett and me to the party.

15. The table is set for us.

16. We are too late to see the first show.

17. They will be happy to come along.

18. Clams and turtles have shells. They are protected by them.

DAY 16

Complete each sentence with the correct word from the parentheses.

19. The baseball game went _____ for the Spartans right from the first inning. (well, better, best)

20. The first batter, Monroe, always hits _____ . (well, better, best)

21. Monroe runs the bases _____ than most players on his team. (well, better, best)

22. Stanley, the second batter, usually hits even _____ than Monroe. (well, better, best)

23. The pitcher threw his _____ pitches to Stanley. (well, better, best)

24. Stanley hit the ball _____ , and it flew over the fence for a two-run home run. (well, better, best)

25. Things went _____ for the Tigers in the second half of the game than in the first. (badly, worse, worst)

Catch and Stretch

Did you know that a backyard game of catch can improve your flexibility? Find a friend or family member and a variety of balls, such as a tennis ball, baseball, softball, or foam ball. Throw each ball back and forth. As you throw, concentrate on extending your front foot and throwing arm. As this gets easier, increase the distance between you and your partner. For a challenge, try throwing with your other hand. This will be harder, but it will give both sides of your body equal stretching time. As you throw, remember to "stretch" your limits!

FACTOID: Nepal is the only country to have a national flag that is not a rectangle.

* See page ii.

PLACE STICKER HERE

Read the story. Then, write four details from the story in the order that they occurred.

Quinn and Phillip washed their dad's car. First, they filled a bucket with soapy water. Quinn got some old rags from the house while Phillip got the hose. They put soapy water all over the car and wiped off the dirt. Next, they rinsed the car with water. To finish the job, Quinn and Phillip dried the car with some clean towels. They were both surprised when their dad gave them $5 each.

1. _____

2. _____

3. _____

4. _____

Each word below contains the suffix *-est*, *-tion*, or *-ty*. Circle each suffix. Then, write the base word.

EXAMPLE:

safe(ty)_____**safe**_____

5. saddest _____

6. hungriest _____

7. preparation _____

8. invention _____

9. tasty _____

10. certainty _____

11. loyalty _____

12. direction _____

13. suggestion _____

14. loveliest _____

15. surest _____

Read the passage. Then, answer the questions.

Lucy Maud Montgomery

Lucy Maud Montgomery is famous for creating the character of Anne Shirley in the Anne of Green Gables series. Montgomery was born in 1874 on Prince Edward Island in Canada. She lived with her grandparents and went to class in a one-room schoolhouse. Her first poem was published when she was 17 years old. She wrote *Anne of Green Gables* in 1905, but it was not published until 1908. The book became a best-seller, and Montgomery wrote several other books based on the main character. Two films and at least seven TV shows have been made from the Anne of Green Gables series. Although Montgomery moved away from Prince Edward Island in 1911, all but one of her books are set there. Many people still visit the island today to see where Anne Shirley grew up.

16. What is the main idea of this passage?
    A. Lucy Maud Montgomery grew up on Prince Edward Island.
    B. Lucy Maud Montgomery is famous for writing *Anne of Green Gables*.
    C. Lucy Maud Montgomery was a schoolteacher.

17. Who is Anne Shirley? _____

18. What was Montgomery's early life like?_____

_____

19. When was Montgomery's first poem published?_____

20. How can you tell that *Anne of Green Gables* was a popular book?

_____

21. Why do many people visit Prince Edward Island today?

_____

FITNESS FLASH: Do arm circles for 30 seconds.

* See page ii.

PLACE STICKER HERE

Multiply to find each product.

1. 16 × 5   2. 15 × 6   3. 28 × 3   4. 24 × 4   5. 26 × 3

6. 47 × 2   7. 19 × 4   8. 19 × 5   9. 38 × 2   10. 21 × 4

Write the past-tense form of each underlined verb.

11. A tadpole <u>hatches</u> from an egg in a pond. _____

12. He <u>looks</u> like a small fish at first. _____

13. The tadpole <u>uses</u> his tail to swim. _____

14. He <u>breathes</u> with gills. _____

15. His appearance <u>changes</u> after a few weeks. _____

16. He <u>starts</u> to grow hind legs. _____

17. His head <u>flattens</u>. _____

18. His gills <u>vanish</u>. _____

19. His tail <u>disappears</u>. _____

20. He <u>hops</u> onto dry land. _____

DAY 18

Follow the directions using a dictionary. The dictionary can be a physical dictionary or online dictionary.

21. Browse through the letter H. Choose a word to write. _____

22. Write the meaning of the word word you chose. _____

_____

23. How many syllables does your word have? _____

24. What mark is used to show how words are divided into syllables? _____

Complete each sentence with the correct form of *good* or *bad* from the parentheses.

25. The weatherperson said that we will have _____ weather on Thursday. (good, better, best)

26. She said that the weather this weekend will be _____ than today. (good, better, best)

27. Sunday will have the _____ weather this week. (good, better, best)

28. Parts of the country are having _____ storms. (bad, worse, worst)

29. The weatherperson is predicting that the_____ of the snow is coming soon. (bad, worse, worst)

30. Florida usually has _____ weather in the winter. (good, better, best)

FACTOID: If the sun were hollow, it could hold more than one million Earths inside it.

PLACE STICKER HERE

Read the passage. Then, answer the questions.

Elisha Otis

Have you ever ridden in an elevator? Elevators make it much easier for people to get from one floor to another in a tall building. At one time, elevators were not as safe as they are today. Elisha Otis helped change that. Early elevators used ropes that sometimes broke, sending the people riding the elevator to the ground. To make elevators safer, Otis made wooden guide rails to go on each side of an elevator. Cables ran through the rails and were connected to a spring that would pull the elevator up if the cables broke. Otis displayed his invention for the first time at the New York Crystal Palace Exhibition in 1853. His safety elevators were used in buildings as tall as the Eiffel Tower in Paris, France, and the Empire State Building in New York City, New York. Otis died in 1861. His sons, Charles and Norton, continued to sell his design, and many elevators today still have the Otis name on them.

1. What is the main idea of this passage?
    A. The Otis family still sells elevators today.
    B. At one time, elevators were unsafe to use.
    C. Elisha Otis found a way to make elevators safe.

2. Why were early elevators dangerous? _____

    _____

3. What did the spring in Otis's elevators do?_____

    _____

4. When and where was Otis's elevator displayed for the first time?_____

5. What are two buildings that used Otis's elevator design?_____

    _____

6. What did Otis's sons do after his death? _____

    _____

DAY 19

Time yourself as you solve the problems. Can you answer them correctly in one minute?

7. 9 × 7 = _____

8. 4 × 6 = _____

9. 8 × 5 = _____

10. 2 × 9 = _____

11. 5 × 3 = _____

12. 8 × 8 = _____

13. 6 × 9 = _____

14. 3 × 7 = _____

15. 5 × 4 = _____

16. 7 × 7 = _____

17. 6 × 8 = _____

18. 4 × 4 = _____

Fill in the blanks to complete the friendly letter. Use correct capitalization.

_____ (date)

_____, (greeting)

I'm having a _____ summer. So far, the best part of the summer has been

_____

_____

_____

_____ , (closing)

_____ (your name)

FITNESS FLASH: Do 10 shoulder shrugs.

* See page ii.

PLACE STICKER HERE

Add to find each sum.

1.   78
      81
    + 65

2.   51
      21
    + 83

3.   81
      57
    + 52

4.   76
      59
    + 53

5.   34
      67
    + 24

6.   76
      53
    + 19

7.   49
      74
    + 84

8.   76
      34
    + 51

9.   28
      54
    + 84

10.   48
      78
    + 28

Read each verb. Write *A* if it is a present-tense action verb. Write *L* if it is a linking verb.

EXAMPLE:

___A___ bloom   ___L___ is

11. _____ has   12. _____ hatch

13. _____ have   14. _____ seem

15. _____ pretend   16. _____ stir

17. _____ becomes   18. _____ study

19. _____ walk   20. _____ hold

21. _____ were   22. _____ am

23. _____ skip   24. _____ was

DAY 20

Divide to find each quotient.

25. 2)84   26. 2)62   27. 2)68   28. 3)93

29. 7)70   30. 5)55   31. 3)69   32. 9)99

33. 3)36   34. 9)90   35. 3)42   36. 4)80

Read each set of sentences. Write *P* next to sentences in the past tense, *PR* next to sentences in the present tense, and *F* next to sentences in the future tense.

37.   A.   Mischa ran to the market. _____

        B.   Mischa will run around the block. _____

        C.   Mischa runs to the park with Lea. _____

38.   A.   I am having green beans with dinner. _____

        B.   I will have corn tomorrow. _____

        C.   I had broccoli yesterday. _____

39.   A.   Troy will catch the ball. _____

        B.   Troy catches the ball. _____

        C.   Troy caught the ball. _____

40.   A.   He will go to the new school. _____

        B.   He went to the new school. _____

        C.   He goes to the new school. _____

PLACE STICKER HERE

Coffee Filter Chromatography

How can colors be separated?

Chromatography is a process used to separate colors. This activity shows how part of the ink in **water-soluble** markers can be dissolved. Other, more soluble colors will travel up a coffee filter with water.

Materials:
- 3 water-soluble markers (not permanent markers)
- 3 drinking glasses
- ruler
- coffee filter
- masking tape
- water
- scissors

Procedure:
Pour water into each glass so that it is about a half-inch (1.3 cm) deep. Label each glass and marker *1, 2,* or *3* using masking tape and the markers. Cut the coffee filter into three strips, one for each marker. Use the water-soluble markers to make one large dot one-third of the way up each coffee filter strip. Do this for all three markers. Place each coffee filter strip in the glass with the same number as the marker. The ink dots should be near, but not under, the water. Let the strips absorb the water.

1. What effect does the water have on the ink dots? _____

    _____

2. What happened differently to each of the three different ink dots? _____

    _____

    _____

3. Which marker's ink traveled the highest on a coffee filter strip? List the other markers in order from highest to lowest._____

    _____

4. What does *water-soluble* mean? _____

5. Which section would you use to find the steps of the experiment?_____

BONUS

Speed Racer

How is the height of a ramp related to the speed of a toy?

Kinetic energy is the energy of motion. *Potential energy* is stored energy, or the energy of position.

Materials:
- ruler
- toy car
- stopwatch
- wooden ramp of any size

Procedure:

Raise one end of the ramp to the lowest height (about 1.5 inches [4 cm]) required for the toy car to roll from one end to the other. Place the car at the top of the ramp, and use the stopwatch to time it as it rolls to the bottom of the ramp. Record the speed of the car and the height of the ramp on the chart below. Repeat the activity two more times, raising the height of the ramp each time.

Trial	Height	Time
1		
2		
3		

1. What is the relationship between the height of the ramp and the speed of the object?_____

2. What surfaces might cause the toy car to roll faster or slower? _____

   _____

3. Try another object, such as a golf or tennis ball. What happens to the speed of the object if it has more mass? _____

4. What is the purpose of the question in bold below the title of the experiment?

   _____

5. How is the graph helpful in organizing the data? _____

   _____

44

Prime Lines

Lines of longitude are imaginary lines that run north to south on a map. They are marked in degrees (°) and help us find locations around the world. The *prime meridian* is the line at 0° longitude. The lines of longitude on a map are measured in 15° segments from the prime meridian. Places east of the prime meridian have the letter *E* after their degrees. Places west of the prime meridian have the letter *W* after their degrees.

Study the map. Then, answer the questions.

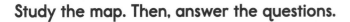

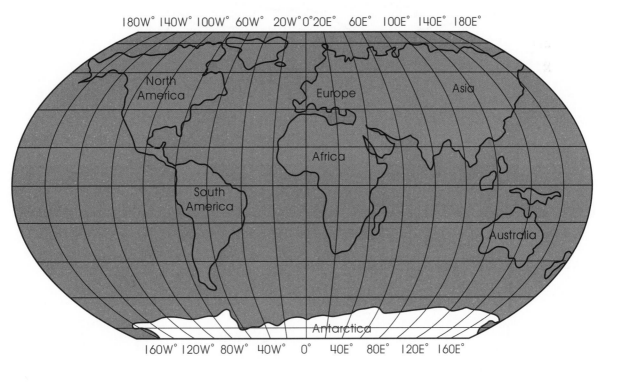

1. The prime meridian is at _____ ° longitude.

2. For locations in South America, the longitude should be followed by the letter _____ .

3. For locations in most of Africa, the longitude should be followed by the letter _____ .

4. Use an orange crayon or marker to trace the prime meridian.

BONUS

Map Scale

A *map scale* represents distance on a map. A map cannot be shown at actual size, so it must be made smaller to fit on paper. On the map below, 1 cm = 100 kilometers.

Study the map of Egypt. Measure the distance between dots with a ruler. Then, change the centimeters to kilometers to find the actual distance between each pair of cities.

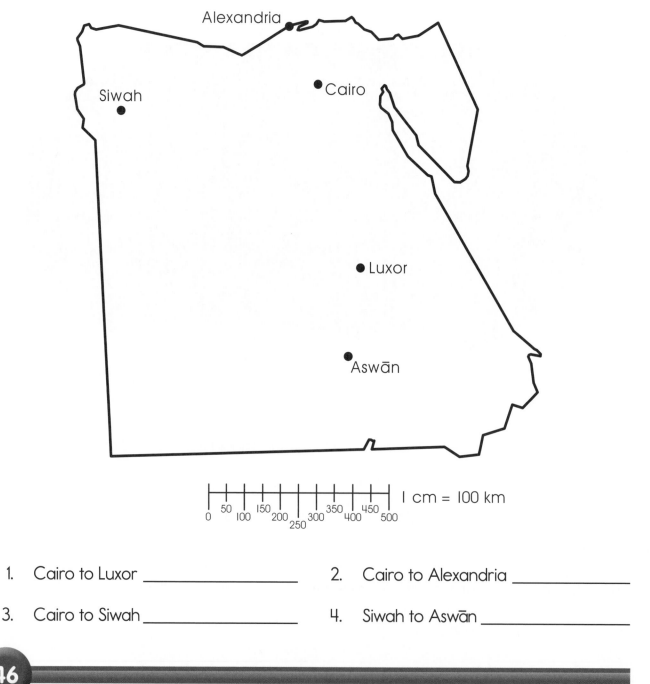

1. Cairo to Luxor _____

2. Cairo to Alexandria _____

3. Cairo to Siwah _____

4. Siwah to Aswān _____

Using a Map

Write the letter of the physical feature next to its name. Use an atlas if you need help.

1. _____ Rocky Mountains

2. _____ Great Lakes

3. _____ Rio Grande

4. _____ Atlantic Ocean

5. _____ Great Salt Lake

6. _____ Great Basin

7. _____ Mississippi River

8. _____ Appalachian Mountains

9. _____ Sierra Nevada Mountains

10. _____ Pacific Ocean

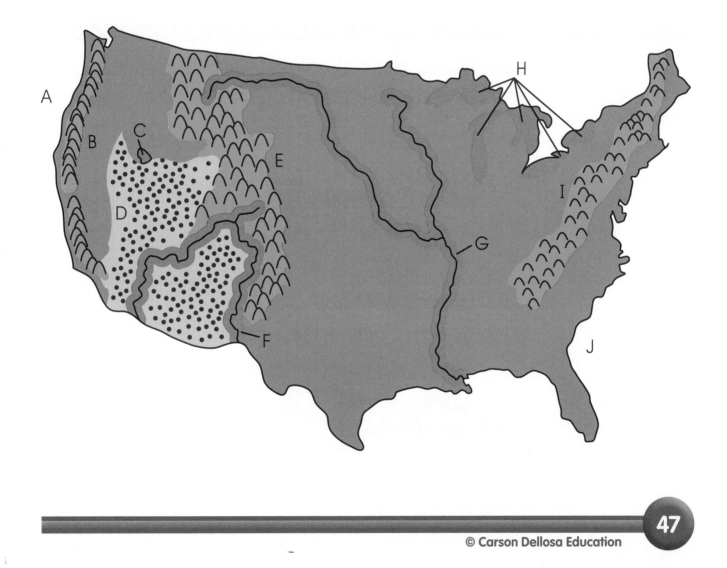

Take It Outside!

Turn your backyard or neighborhood into a math classroom to practice estimation. Put on your gardening gloves and pick up a small clump of grass, wood chips, pine straw, or other safe, small material. Estimate how many pieces are in the group. Then, place the material on the ground and count the number of pieces in it to see how close your estimate was.

Make a relief map of an outdoor space near your home. Wear gardening gloves and use sand, mud, sticks, and other natural materials to form the physical features of the area. Shape the land features on a hard, flat surface, such as a piece of plywood or a sandbox floor. Some of the physical features may not be the usual ones found in your social studies class. Make whatever features are noticeable on the landscape's surface, such as hills, driveways, ponds, and playground equipment.

Gather a variety of natural objects, such as shells, stones, leaves, small sticks, pine straw, and bark. Use glue to attach the objects to a flat, square piece of wood or cardboard to create a natural masterpiece. Make a shape, design, or even a scene to illustrate the beauty of the natural world.

* See page ii.

Monthly Goals

Think of three goals to set for yourself this month. For example, you may want to learn five math facts each week. Write your goals on the lines and review them with an adult.

Place a sticker next to each of your goals that you complete. Feel proud that you have met your goals!

1. _____ PLACE STICKER HERE

2. _____ PLACE STICKER HERE

3. _____ PLACE STICKER HERE

Word List

The following words are used in this section. They are good words for you to know. Read each word. Use a dictionary to look up each word that you do not know. Then, write two sentences. Use a word from the word list in each sentence.

astronomy	improve
choosing	instant
degrees	recreation
demanding	scattered
descriptions	vertically

1. _____

_____

2. _____

_____

Introduction to Strength

This section includes fitness and character development activities that focus on strength. These activities are designed to get you moving and thinking about strengthening your body and your character. If you have limited mobility, feel free to modify any suggested exercises to fit your individual abilities.

Physical Strength

Like flexibility, strength is necessary for you to be healthy. You may think that a strong person is someone who can lift a lot of weight. However, strength is more than the ability to pick up heavy things. Strength is built over time. You are stronger now than you were in kindergarten. What are some activities that you can do now that you could not do then?

You can gain strength through everyday activities and many fun exercises. Carry grocery bags to build your arms. Ride a bike to strengthen your legs. Swim to strengthen your whole body. Exercises such as push-ups and chin-ups are also great strength builders.

Set goals this summer to improve your strength. Base your goals on activities you enjoy. Talk about your goals with an adult. As you meet your goals, set new ones. Celebrate your stronger, healthier body!

Strength of Character

As you build your physical strength, work on your inner strength, too. Having a strong character means standing up for who you are, even if others do not agree with your point of view.

You can show inner strength in many ways, such as being honest, standing up for someone who needs your help, and putting your best efforts into every task. It is not always easy to show inner strength. Can you think of a time when you used inner strength to handle a situation, such as being teased by another child at the park?

Improve your inner strength over the summer. Think about ways you can show strength of character, such as showing respect for everyone playing a sport, win or lose. Reflect on your positive growth. Be proud of your strong character!

Draw a line to match each related division and multiplication problem.

1.	$65 \div 5$	A.	9×4	9.	$72 \div 9$	A.	18×4
2.	$24 \div 6$	B.	6×4	10.	$38 \div 2$	B.	8×9
3.	$36 \div 9$	C.	9×5	11.	$72 \div 4$	C.	22×4
4.	$45 \div 5$	D.	17×3	12.	$50 \div 2$	D.	19×2
5.	$28 \div 7$	E.	7×4	13.	$56 \div 4$	E.	43×2
6.	$64 \div 8$	F.	9×9	14.	$86 \div 2$	F.	25×2
7.	$51 \div 3$	G.	8×8	15.	$88 \div 4$	G.	14×4
8.	$81 \div 9$	H.	13×5	16.	$75 \div 3$	H.	25×3

Write a book report about your favorite book. Use the outline to help you.

Title _____

Author _____

Main characters _____

Where and when does the story take place? _____

What is the main theme of the book? _____

_____

Why did you like the book? _____

_____

_____

DAY 1

Quotation marks set off what someone says. Write quotation marks in each sentence around what each person says.

EXAMPLE:

Uncle Neil said, "I will pack a picnic lunch."

17. Where is the big beach ball? asked Jeff.

18. Ilene exclaimed, That is a wonderful idea!

19. Come and do your work, Grandma said, or you can't go with us.

20. Yesterday, said Ella, I saw a pretty robin in the tree by my window.

21. I will always take care of my pets, promised Theodore.

22. Rachel said, Maybe we should have practiced more.

23. Dr. Jacobs asked, How are you, Pat?

On a separate sheet of paper, write a story about a real or imaginary place you would like to visit this summer.

Consider the following questions before you begin to write.

- Who are the characters in the story?

- Where does the story take place?

- How does the story begin?

- What happens next?

- How does the story end?

FACTOID: Humans have kept dogs as pets for about 10,000 years.

PLACE
STICKER
HERE

Do you think that students should have to wear school uniforms? Why or why not? State your opinion and provide reasons that support it.

_____

_____

_____

_____

_____

_____

_____

_____

Common nouns are general names for people, places, or things. *Proper nouns* name specific people, places, or things and begin with uppercase letters. Write each noun under the correct heading.

	Common Nouns	Proper Nouns
Monday	_____	_____
ocean		
class	_____	_____
November		
holiday	_____	_____
July		
boat	_____	_____
beans		
Rex	_____	_____
North Carolina		

DAY 2

Read the passage. Then, answer the questions.

Choosing a Pet

Before you decide what kind of pet you would like to own, there are some things you should think about. First, find out how much care the pet will need. Dogs need to be walked; horses need to be exercised; cats need a place to scratch. All pets need to be kept clean and well fed. You should also think about where your pet would live. Big pets need a lot of room, while little pets do not need as much room.

1. What is the topic of the passage?
   A. caring for a dog
   C. feeding big pets
   B. choosing a pet
   D. where pets live

2. What is the main idea?
   A. finding good homes for pets
   C. things to think about before choosing a pet
   B. things to do when choosing a pet
   D. bring your pet home

Write the correct homophone from the word bank to complete each sentence.

too	two	to	cent	scent	sent

3. The _____ kittens played with the ball.

4. A penny equals one _____ .

5. My aunt asked me to go _____ the store.

6. Malcolm _____ a letter to his friend.

7. I will clean my desk and the table _____.

8. The flower has a sweet _____ .

FITNESS FLASH: Do 10 lunges.

* See page ii.

Write the prefix *re-* or *un-* in each blank to complete each sentence. On the line, write the meaning of the new word.

1. Please _____move your shoes before you come in. _____

2. That was an _____usual movie. _____

3. I would like to _____new the magazine subscription. _____

4. That was an _____common rainstorm. _____

5. You will have to _____tell the story later. _____

A *pronoun* is a word that takes the place of a noun. Read each sentence. Then, circle the noun(s) that each underlined pronoun is replacing.

EXAMPLE:

Betty has a (computer.) She keeps <u>it</u> on her desk.

6. Liv forgot her umbrella. She went home to get <u>it</u>.

7. Benji asked Juan if <u>he</u> would teach him to hit a baseball.

8. Amira and Becca both collect seashells. Sometimes, <u>they</u> trade with each other.

9. Rachel plays the violin, and sometimes <u>she</u> sings, too.

10. We gave our dog a new toy. Fido barked when he saw <u>it</u>.

11. Our school bus is always crowded, and <u>it</u> is usually noisy, too.

DAY 3

Read each group of words. Circle each correctly spelled word and write it on the line.

12. wunderful   wonderful   wondirful   _____

13. warm   wirm   warme   _____

14. wurried   woried   worried   _____

15. woh   hwo   who   _____

16. wair   where   wher   _____

17. weigh   weh   wiegh   _____

18. wint   wat   want   _____

19. w'ont   won't   wo'nt   _____

Tug-of-War Trials

Play tug-of-war. Tie several sturdy pieces of fabric together to make a "rope." Be sure to use a red piece of fabric in the middle. Use a ruler or other straight object to place a line on the ground. Group a few friends or family members into teams. Have each team member get ready at her rope position. Then, have them start pulling on the rope at the same time until one team pulls the other across the line. Change the teams. When everyone is done showing her strength, celebrate as a group with refreshing glasses of lemonade.

FACTOID: The U.S. Library of Congress has more than 168 million items.

* See page ii.

PLACE STICKER HERE

Name each figure by its points and label it with the correct symbol.

EXAMPLES:

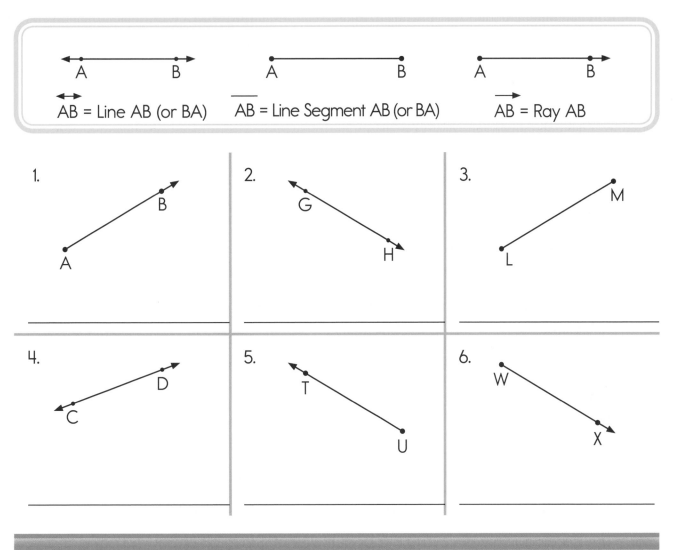

What would you do if you woke up with green hair?

_____

_____

_____

_____

DAY 4

Write the correct homophone from the parentheses to complete each sentence.

7. Asha has two _____ and three oranges. (pears, pairs)

8. Brian can never _____ to play the game right. (seam, seem)

9. Mother will sift the _____ for the cookies. (flour, flower)

10. I hope that I can get everything _____ on time. (write, right)

11. Nannette _____ the baking contest. (won, one)

12. The bread _____ was very sticky. (doe, dough)

Context clues are the words around a word you do not know. Use context clues to figure out the meaning of each underlined word. Then, circle the letter next to the word's correct meaning.

13. My brother and I often <u>argue</u> about who gets to use the computer.
    A. work   B. disagree   C. study

14. The <u>official</u> told us not to enter the building until 8 o'clock.
    A. person in charge   B. nurse   C. child

15. Josie saw an <u>unusual</u> light in the sky and asked her father what it was.
    A. dark   B. star   C. different

16. The <u>cardinal</u> in my backyard is a beautiful sight. I love his bright red color and sweet song.
    A. singer   B. branch   C. bird with red feathers

17. Mom asked me to turn down the <u>volume</u> on the TV because it was too loud.
    A. noise level   B. book   C. color

FITNESS FLASH: Do five push-ups.

* See page ii.

PLACE STICKER HERE

Use the clock to answer each question.

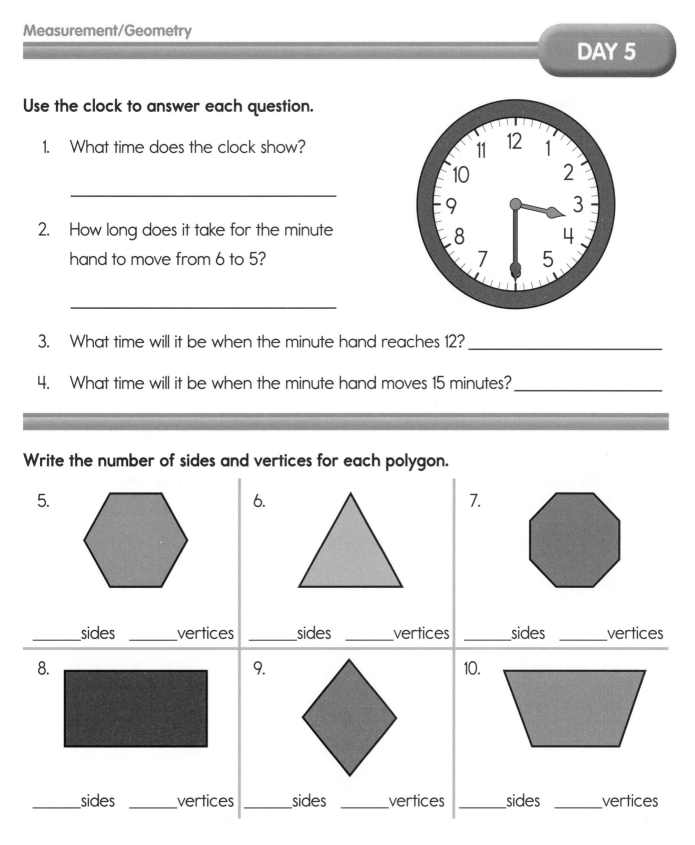

1. What time does the clock show?

   _____

2. How long does it take for the minute hand to move from 6 to 5?

   _____

3. What time will it be when the minute hand reaches 12? _____

4. What time will it be when the minute hand moves 15 minutes? _____

Write the number of sides and vertices for each polygon.

5.

_____sides _____vertices

6.

_____sides _____vertices

7.

_____sides _____vertices

8.

_____sides _____vertices

9.

_____sides _____vertices

10.

_____sides _____vertices

11. Which three shapes have the same number of sides and vertices ?

   _____   _____   _____

DAY 5

Add to find each sum.

12.	4,340 5,433 +3,238	13.	356 674 +380	14.	54 39 +73	15.	634 198 +518	16.	67 98 +74

17.	47 34 +99	18.	321 436 +548	19.	2,783 2,546 +6,748	20.	9,418 8,009 +7,245	21.	4,259 1,564 +2,873

An *adverb* is a word that modifies a verb. Circle the adverb in each sentence. Then, underline the verb that the adverb modifies.

22. On Independence Day, we usually go to the parade.

23. We drive slowly because of traffic.

24. The parade often begins with a marching band.

25. The marching band plays loudly.

26. The huge crowd cheers excitedly.

27. My favorite part is when the big floats pass near us.

28. All of the floats are decorated beautifully.

29. We never see one we don't like.

CHARACTER CHECK: Think about an area in your life that you would like to improve. Set a goal for yourself.

PLACE STICKER HERE

Complete each multiplication chart.

1.

× 2	
4	
8	
3	6
6	
9	
5	10
7	

2.

× 3	
3	9
7	
5	
2	
6	18
4	
8	

3.

× 4	
10	
5	20
8	
4	
7	
6	
9	

4.

× 5	
9	
2	
6	
3	15
5	
7	
4	

Write the correct word from the word bank to complete each sentence.

cottage

quarter

curtains

circus

bell

pictures

pennies

market

chatter

5. Look at all of the funny _____ in this book.

6. You can buy bread and milk at the _____.

7. We live in a small _____.

8. This pencil costs a _____.

9. I am saving a lot of _____ in a jar.

10. The clowns at the _____ were great.

11. When you hear the _____, run fast.

12. We have white _____ on our windows.

13. Chipmunks _____ .

DAY 6

Divide to find each quotient.

14. 6)360   15. 8)432   16. 4)496   17. 7)637

18. 8)856   19. 7)105   20. 9)720   21. 7)196

Write the correct past-tense form of the irregular verb in parentheses to complete each sentence.

22. Our teacher _____ our class a book about insects. (read)

23. I _____ Mr. Lee before he was my teacher. (know)

24. Ms. Kemp _____ us that we could eat outside today. (tell)

25. Drew _____ that I can borrow his jump rope anytime. (say)

26. I _____ a bird chirping in a tree. (hear)

27. Cody _____ a new baseball glove today. (buy)

28. Hannah _____ her favorite blue shirt under her bed. (find)

29. Brooke and Gene each _____ an apple for a snack. (eat)

30. Jaime and her dad _____ a bookcase for her room. (build)

FACTOID: The largest recorded prairie dog town was located in Texas. It covered about 25,000 square miles (65,000 square kilometers).

PLACE STICKER HERE

Draw a straight line through three numbers that, when added together, total each sum provided.

1. Sum: 78

20	28	14
16	32	42
19	18	13

2. Sum: 110

16	33	64
39	22	44
51	10	72

3. Sum: 251

71	47	18
82	20	46
98	43	33

4. Sum: 149

15	93	24
63	25	33
63	25	61

5. Sum: 506

94	100	90
88	206	58
79	200	96

6. Sum: 189

94	100	90
88	20	58
79	10	96

Write the correct past- or present-tense form of the verb in parentheses to complete each sentence.

7. My friends and I like to _____ clay animals. (make)

8. Yesterday, we _____ the clay into different shapes. (roll)

9. Jeremy _____ making a clay hippo yesterday. (enjoy)

10. Our teacher _____ us bake the clay animals. (help)

11. He always _____ them in the kiln. (place)

12. After they were baked and cooled, we _____ them. (paint)

13. Often, we _____ them as gifts. (give)

DAY 7

Read each group of words. Write the words in the correct order to make complete sentences. Use correct punctuation and capitalization.

14.   rode hill the I down on bike a _____

_____

15.   garden a our mom backyard I planted and in my _____

_____

16.   themselves elephants animals when braced all the sneezed the of _____

_____

17.   bottles of full wagon a pulled cory _____

_____

Find the area of each shape.

18.

area = _____ square units

19.

area = _____ square units

20.

area = _____ square units

21.

area = _____ square units

PLACE STICKER HERE

Add commas where they belong in each phrase or sentence.

1. My family visits Spring Grove Minnesota every year in the summer.

2. Dear Grandpa

3. Yours truly

4. On October 9 2009 Carolyn saw the play.

5. My aunt and uncle live in North Branch New York.

6. Dear Jon

7. January 1 2010

8. Paris Texas is located in the northeastern part of the state.

Circle the measurement from the parentheses that correctly completes each sentence.

9. A bathtub could hold up to (150 milliliters, 150 liters) of water.

10. A flower vase could hold up to (1 liter, 1 milliliter) of water.

11. A bike would weigh (10 grams, 10 kilograms).

12. An orange would weigh (100 grams, 100 ounces).

13. An ear of corn would be (11 inches, 11 yards) long.

14. A pencil would be (15 meters, 15 centimeters) long.

DAY 8

Divide to find each quotient.

15. 2)184

16. 7)210

17. 7)231

18. 5)625

19. 9)459

20. 4)256

21. 9)144

22. 5)355

23. 9)162

24. 8)320

25. 6)132

26. 8)136

Demanding Up-Downs

There are many great exercises to improve your strength. One that uses your entire body is called an *up-down*. Begin by running in place. Then, drop to the ground with your chest to the floor and your legs straight behind you. Do one push-up. Then, jump back to your feet and run in place again. Remember to start slowly. Although it is not easy, doing up-downs is a great way to improve your overall fitness.

FACTOID: Cheetahs are the only cats that do not have fully retractable claws.

* See page ii.

PLACE STICKER HERE

Answer each question.

1. How many 6s are in 18? _____

2. How many 9s are in 18? _____

3. How many 5s are in 25? _____

4. How many 7s are in 21? _____

5. How many 2s are in 8? _____

6. How many 8s are in 32? _____

7. How many 4s are in 20? _____

8. How many 6s are in 36? _____

Read each sentence. If the underlined word is spelled correctly, write *correct.* **If it is spelled incorrectly, rewrite the word with the correct spelling.**

9. I'd like a glass of water. _____

10. Do you know where they've been today? _____

11. Be carefull with that knife. _____

12. My mom was very unhappy today. _____

13. What did Joni plant in her gardin? _____

14. We looked at all of the babyies in the hospital. _____

15. Aunt Mary canned 10 pounds of cherries. _____

16. He waved at us from the window. _____

17. Did you like the new movee? _____

18. Remember to set your alarm clock. _____

FITNESS FLASH: Do 10 squats.

* See page ii.

Read the story. Then, answer the questions.

Good Friends

Robert and Kaye are two of my best friends. We have gone to school together since we were in kindergarten. We even go to summer camp and the recreation center together. There are many reasons why I like to spend time with them. Robert always lets me borrow his skateboard. He knows that if I had a skateboard, I would let him borrow it. Robert is a person I can count on, too. When we are out riding our bikes together, Kaye sometimes lets me ride in front while she rides behind me. She understands that one way to be a good friend is by taking turns and being fair.

19. How is Robert a good friend?_____

_____

20. Is Kaye a fair person? Why? _____

_____

21. List three things that the friends do together. _____

_____

22. Write a few sentences about what you think makes a good friend.

_____

_____

_____

_____

23. What does it mean to say you can "count on" someone?_____

_____

_____

Solve each word problem. Show your work.

1. There are 48 people coming to a family reunion. One fourth of them live out of state. How many live in-state?

2. At the reunion, 3 meals will be served. Each person will use one plate for each meal. How many plates are needed?

3. The oldest person coming to the reunion is 84. The youngest person is 3. How many times older is the oldest person than the youngest person?

4. Of the people coming to the reunion, 16 are children. Each child will get 8 water balloons. How many water balloons are needed?

Read each pair of words. For each pair, write one way the two things are alike and one way they are different.

5. leopard, cheetah _____

_____

6. keyboard, piano _____

_____

7. cabin, tent _____

_____

8. whistle, sing _____

_____

DAY 10

Subtract to find each difference.

9. 943
− 549

10. 7,452
− 6,789

11. 526
− 268

12. 526
− 498

13. 754
− 528

14. 751
− 439

15. 8,236
− 5,548

16. 7,840
− 4,251

17. 6,324
− 3,489

18. 7,223
− 1,759

In the sentences below, circle the helping verbs. Underline the main verbs.

19. Antonio is going to soccer practice tomorrow.

20. The girls were planning a sleepover for Friday.

21. Samir has read that book at least three times.

22. Mom and Dad were expecting you for dinner.

23. Colin has used that same duffel bag for the last five years.

24. Brandy will bring snacks to the game.

25. Zara is joining the French club.

26. Tonight, we are studying for the quiz at Annie's house.

CHARACTER CHECK: Look up the word *responsibility* in a dictionary. Then, write three ways that you can be responsible.

PLACE STICKER HERE

Add to find each sum.

1. 6,898
   5,433
   + 2,154

2. 8,459
   4,908
   + 4,356

3. 525
   653
   + 896

4. 5,265
   2,278
   + 8,365

5. 2,147
   3,255
   + 2,256

6. 654
   452
   + 138

7. 7,092
   5,405
   + 6,124

8. 5,768
   6,937
   + 7,034

9. 4,265
   5,124
   + 6,489

10. 8,214
    7,716
    + 6,389

A *metaphor* is a figure of speech in which two things are compared without using the words *like* or *as*. Read each metaphor. Write the names of the two things that are being compared.

11. The falling snowflakes were tiny dancers whirling through the sky.

    _____ and _____

12. The highway was a parking lot, and it took us hours to get home.

    _____ and _____

13. The tornado was a powerful train heading straight for the tiny town.

    _____ and _____

14. Excitement was an electrical current that pulsed through the audience.

    _____ and _____

15. Dara's fingers were icicles after two hours of sledding.

    _____ and _____

DAY 11

Write a number for each expanded form.

EXAMPLE:

	16.	17.	18.
7,000 + 500 + 60 + 2	1,000 + 800 + 40 + 7	4,000 + 200 + 80	9,000 + 900 + 90 + 9
_____7,562_____	_____	_____	_____
19.	20.	21.	22.
7,000 + 60 + 8	800 + 50 + 5	6,000 + 800 + 4	5,000 + 400 + 30 + 2
_____	_____	_____	_____

Use the words from the word bank to solve the crossword puzzle.

Across

23. very sure

24. to make something look larger

25. to go behind

26. something that needs to be done now

27. to care for the sick

Down

28. to spin

29. to send back

30. not better

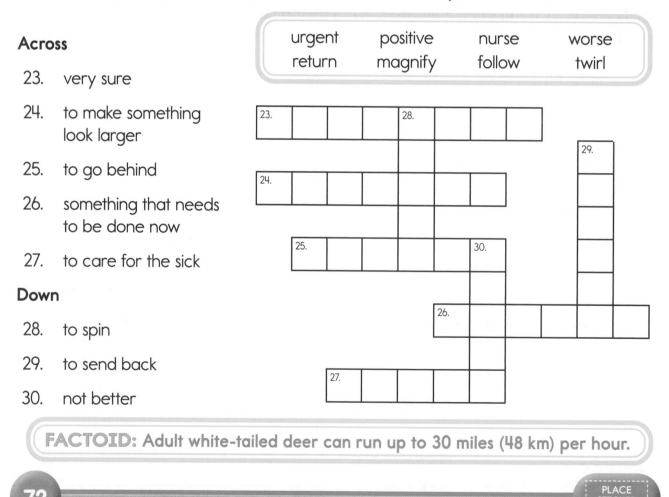

urgent	positive	nurse	worse
return	magnify	follow	twirl

FACTOID: Adult white-tailed deer can run up to 30 miles (48 km) per hour.

PLACE STICKER HERE

Write each number. Then, write its expanded form.

1. five hundred sixty-one _____

2. four hundred eighty-six _____

3. four thousand eight hundred twenty-six _____

Count how many are in each set. Write each number.

4.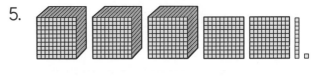

5.

_____

_____

Write the letter of each definition next to the correct geometry term.

6. _____ parallel lines

7. _____ perpendicular lines

8. _____ vertex

9. _____ face

10. _____ edge

11. _____ ray

12. _____ line segment

13. _____ angle

14. _____ intersecting lines

A. a line with one endpoint that continues in one direction

B. the endpoint of three line segments on a solid figure

C. a flat surface of a solid figure

D. where two or more faces of a solid figure meet

E. lines that intersect to form four right angles

F. the space between two nonparallel rays that share an endpoint

G. lines that cross at only one point

H. a line with two endpoints

I. lines that never intersect

Read the story. Then, answer the questions.

Tara found a pair of pink sunglasses on the bus. They had red lightning bolts on the earpieces. Tara liked them. After lunch, she put on the sunglasses to wear at recess. A girl ran to her and said, "Excuse me, but I think those are mine." Tara's heart sank.

15. What do you think Tara will do? _____

_____

16. Which clues helped you decide? _____

_____

Rewrite the paragraph with the correct punctuation and capitalization.

last summer we went camping in colorado we went hiking and swimming every day one time i actually saw a baby white-tailed deer with spots we also took photos of a lot of pretty rocks flowers and leaves we had a great time i didn't want to leave

_____

_____

_____

_____

_____

_____

FITNESS FLASH: Do five push-ups.

* See page ii.

PLACE STICKER HERE

Use a protractor to measure each angle. Write each angle measurement. Then, write *right*, *straight*, *acute*, or *obtuse* to identify each angle.

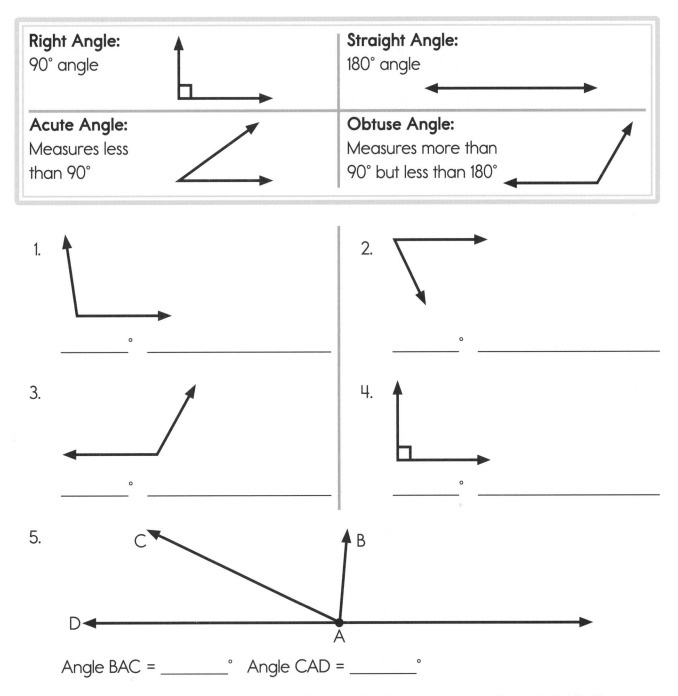

Right Angle:
90° angle

Straight Angle:
180° angle

Acute Angle:
Measures less than 90°

Obtuse Angle:
Measures more than 90° but less than 180°

1. _____° _____

2. _____° _____

3. _____° _____

4. _____° _____

5.

Angle BAC = _____° Angle CAD = _____°

Add the measures of angles BAC and CAD to find the measure of angle BAD. Use your answers above to complete the equation:

_____° + _____° = _____°

Read the directions from the oatmeal box. Then, answer the questions.

> ### Instant Oatmeal
> 1. Empty the package into a microwave-safe bowl.
> 2. Add $\frac{2}{3}$ cup (156 mL) water and stir.
> 3. Microwave on high for 1 to 2 minutes; stir.
> 4. Pour some milk on top if desired.
> 5. Let cool; eat with a spoon.

6. What do the directions tell you how to make?

    A.   oatmeal   B.   instant oatmeal   C.   cold cereal

7. What is the first step? _____

8. What materials do you need? _____

    _____

9. How long should it take to make this?

    A.   a few seconds   B.   a few minutes   C.   30 minutes

---

Compare each set of numbers. Write < (less than) or > (greater than) on each line.

10. 126 _____ 261   11. 999 _____ 899   12. 126 _____ 226

13. 342 _____ 231   14. 524 _____ 624   15. 524 _____ 624

16. 619 _____ 719   17. 267 _____ 367   18. 580 _____ 579

19. 1,638 _____ 738   20. 4,206 _____ 5,206   21. 3,487 _____ 3,748

FACTOID: Angel Falls in Venezuela is the tallest waterfall on Earth at 3,212 feet (979 meters).

PLACE STICKER HERE

Display the data on the line plot.

Plant	A	B	C	D	E	F	G	H	I	J
Inches grown	$\frac{1}{4}$	$\frac{3}{4}$	$\frac{1}{4}$	$\frac{2}{4}$	$\frac{1}{4}$	$\frac{1}{4}$	$\frac{3}{4}$	$\frac{4}{4}$	$\frac{4}{4}$	$\frac{1}{4}$

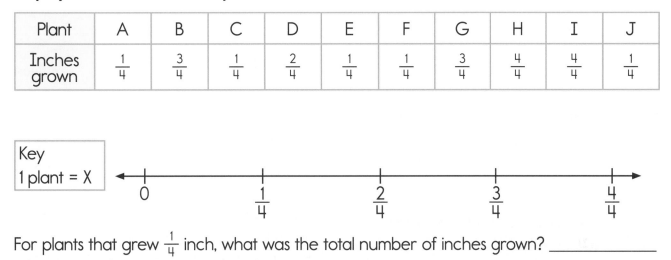

Key
1 plant = X

For plants that grew $\frac{1}{4}$ inch, what was the total number of inches grown? _____

Write a prepositional phrase to complete each sentence. Begin each phrase with a preposition from the box.

across	by	inside	over	under
beside	behind	on	to	up

EXAMPLE: Lex received a letter in the mail ____from his Grandma____ .

1. Maggie found her brother hiding _____.

2. It was hot outside, so we decided to have the picnic _____ .

3. Liza walked _____ and picked a juicy tomato for lunch.

4. Donita's legs were tired from the long hike _____ .

5. I left your books _____ .

6. Mr. Juarez put the plant _____ , where it would get lots of light.

7. Tomas sat _____ in the cafeteria.

8. The cardinal flew _____ and landed on a branch.

DAY 14

Study the table of contents. Then, answer the questions.

9. On what page should you start reading to learn about writing a story?

    _____

10. On what page should you start reading to learn about commas?

    _____

11. On what page should you start reading to learn how to describe what something looks like?

    _____

Shade the models to represent each fraction. If the fractions are equal, write = on the line. If they are not equal, write ≠.

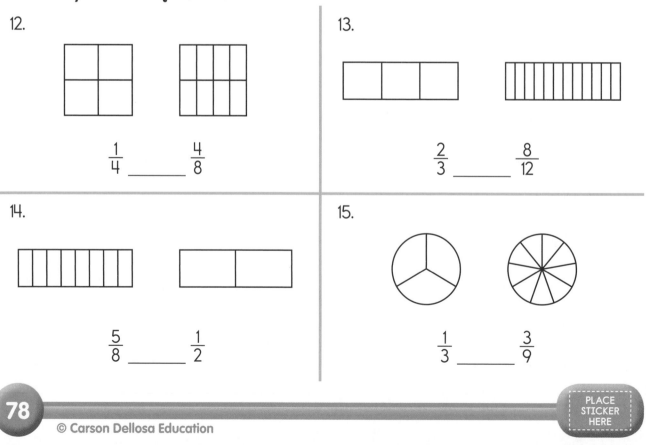

12.

$\frac{1}{4}$ _____ $\frac{4}{8}$

13.

$\frac{2}{3}$ _____ $\frac{8}{12}$

14.

$\frac{5}{8}$ _____ $\frac{1}{2}$

15.

$\frac{1}{3}$ _____ $\frac{3}{9}$

PLACE STICKER HERE

Solve each problem. Show your work.

1. Mai rode her bike 2 miles. There are 5,280 feet in 1 mile. How many feet did Mai ride her bike?

_____ feet

2. 78 boxes were loaded into a truck. Each box weighed 9 pounds. How many pounds were loaded into the truck?

_____ pounds

3. A pool holds 4,800 gallons of water. How many hours will it take to fill the pool if 120 gallons of water are added each hour?

_____ hours

4. A broadcasting tower will be 2,542 feet tall when it is completed. So far, the builders have constructed 1,268 feet of the tower. How many more feet do the builders have to go?

_____ feet

Write an ending to the story.

The three friends had not seen Logan for a long time. They were standing in the main room of the natural history museum. "He was here a little while ago," said Kim. The museum was closing. Most of the other visitors had already left.

"Logan likes the dinosaur exhibit and the astronomy room," said Craig. "Maybe we should go look there."

Just then, a museum guard said, "Sorry, but the museum is closing. You'll have to come back tomorrow."

_____

_____

_____

_____

Circle the equation you could use to solve each word problem.

5.   A 65-story building is 780 feet tall. How tall is a 42-story building?
 A.   (65 – 42) × 780 = ?
 B.   (780 ÷ 65) × 42 = ?
 C.   (65 × 42) ÷ 780 = ?
 D.   (780 ÷ ?) + 42 = 65

6.   Mr. Han received 9 boxes of new pencils. Each box contained 12 pencils. If Mr. Han had a total of 86 students, and he gave each student 1 pencil, how many pencils did he have left?
 A.   (86 ÷ 9) – ? = 12
 B.   (? + 12) × 9 = 86
 C.   (12 × 9) – 86 = ?
 D.   (86 ÷ 12) × 9 = ?

7.   The McCrary Theater seats 950 people. There are 400 seats in Section B and 350 seats in Section C. The best seats are in Section A. If all tickets for seating in Section A are sold, the theater collects $3,600. How much does it cost per ticket for seating in Section A?
 A.   3,600 ÷ [950 – (400 + 350)] = ?
 B.   (400 + 350) × 950 ÷ 3,600 = ?
 C.   (3,600 ÷ 950) × (400 + 350) = ?
 D.   3,600 ÷ (950 + 400 + 350) = ?

A *simile* compares two unlike things using the words *like* or *as*. Complete each sentence by making a comparison.

EXAMPLE: The daffodils were as yellow as _____lemons_____ .

8.   The piano keys were as white as _____ .

9.   The fireworks were as bright as the _____ .

10.   His eyes were as green as the _____ .

11.   The balloons were like a bunch of _____ .

12.   Her eyes sparkled like _____ .

13.   The wind was as gentle as _____ .

Draw three lines beneath each letter that should be capitalized.

Jane Goodall

jane goodall was born in 1934 in hampstead, london. She was given a chimpanzee toy named jubilee when she was young. Jane goodall visited the gombe stream national park in Tanzania to study chimpanzees. She later got a degree from the University of cambridge. jane goodall gave the chimpanzees she studied names like fifi and david Greybeard. She has won many awards, including the united nations messenger of peace prize.

The *main idea* tells what a story is about. Underline the sentence in each story that tells the main idea.

1. Penny's dog Coco likes to eat special snacks. Coco eats carrots. She also likes cheese. Her favorite snack is peanut butter dog biscuits. Penny makes sure that Coco does not eat too many snacks. They also go for a walk every afternoon.

2. Oliver Owl is teaching Owen Owl to fly. Oliver tells Owen to perch on the highest branch of the tallest tree. "Then, jump and flap your wings as hard as you can," he says. Owen is nervous, but he trusts Oliver. He jumps from the branch and flaps his wings. Oliver cheers as Owen starts to fly! Later, Owen says that Oliver is good at teaching little owls how to fly.

CHARACTER CHECK: Why is it important to be someone people can trust? Write your answer on a separate sheet of paper.

Difficult Decisions

Self-discipline means making yourself do what you know you should. Showing self-discipline can be difficult. But, it becomes easier with practice.

Read the following situation. On a separate sheet of paper, write the possible consequence of not using self-discipline. Then, write the reward for showing self-discipline.

You have been learning to play guitar, and you have become pretty good. During the school year, you practiced for at least 20 minutes every day. Your lessons start again in August. Sometimes, other activities pop up during the summer, like swimming practice and other fun outdoor activities. Playing guitar every day can seem like a chore when there are other cool things to do.

What is the funniest thing your grandparents or other relatives have told you about another family member? Retell the story.

_____

_____

_____

_____

_____

FACTOID: Baby blue whales can gain up to nine pounds (4.1 kg) per hour, or more than 200 pounds (90.7 kg) per day.

PLACE STICKER HERE

DAY 17

Write *cm*, *m*, or *km* to complete each sentence.

1 meter (m) = 100 centimeters (cm)	1 kilometer (km) = 1,000 meters (m)

1. Reid is 150 _____ tall.

2. Paige's room is 5 _____ wide.

3. Whitney's hand is 14 _____ long and 5 _____ wide.

4. Mr. Suarez drove his car 84 _____ the first hour.

5. The distance from Chicago, Illinois, to Denver, Colorado, is 1,466 _____.

6. Myla's kitchen is approximately 7_____wide.

7. The flagpole at the post office is 46 _____ tall.

8. Lin and Tara walked approximately 3 _____ in 30 minutes.

Compare the fractions. Use the greater than (>), less than (<), or equal to (=) symbols.
Hint: It is easier to compare fractions when their denominators are the same.

EXAMPLE: $\frac{6}{8}$ ⓥ $\frac{2}{4}$ (Think: $\frac{2}{4}$ is equal to $\frac{4}{8}$. I can multiply the numerator and denominator by 2 to change $\frac{2}{4}$ to $\frac{4}{8}$.)

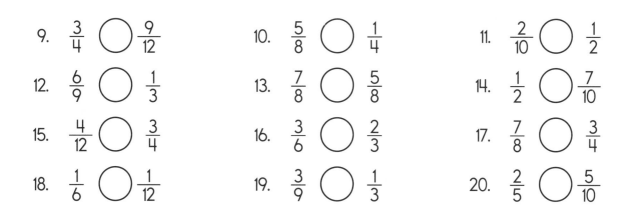

9. $\frac{3}{4}$ ◯ $\frac{9}{12}$

10. $\frac{5}{8}$ ◯ $\frac{1}{4}$

11. $\frac{2}{10}$ ◯ $\frac{1}{2}$

12. $\frac{6}{9}$ ◯ $\frac{1}{3}$

13. $\frac{7}{8}$ ◯ $\frac{5}{8}$

14. $\frac{1}{2}$ ◯ $\frac{7}{10}$

15. $\frac{4}{12}$ ◯ $\frac{3}{4}$

16. $\frac{3}{6}$ ◯ $\frac{2}{3}$

17. $\frac{7}{8}$ ◯ $\frac{3}{4}$

18. $\frac{1}{6}$ ◯ $\frac{1}{12}$

19. $\frac{3}{9}$ ◯ $\frac{1}{3}$

20. $\frac{2}{5}$ ◯ $\frac{5}{10}$

DAY 17

Write an equation to solve each word problem.

21. Sondra read 4 books. Lucas read 5 times as many books. How many books did Lucas read?

22. Company A sold 108 T-shirts at the concert. This amount was 3 times as many as Company B sold. How many T-shirts did Company B sell?

23. If a tree grows 18 inches each year, how many years will it take for the tree to grow 162 inches?

24. For most of the year, a florist sells 7 dozen roses per week. During the week of Valentine's Day, she sells 133 dozen roses. How many times more is this amount than the usual weekly sale?

Read the story. Then, answer the questions.

The children were playing baseball in the empty lot. Brooke was at bat. She swung hard and hit the ball farther than anyone else that day. The ball sailed across the lot and smashed through Ms. Havel's window. Brooke knew that Ms. Havel would be upset. The other children scattered and ran for home. Brooke looked at the broken window. Then, she started walking toward the house.

25. What do you think Brooke will do? _____

_____

26. Which clues helped you decide? _____

_____

FITNESS FLASH: Do 10 sit-ups.

* See page ii.

PLACE STICKER HERE

Solve each equation. Shade the models to help you.

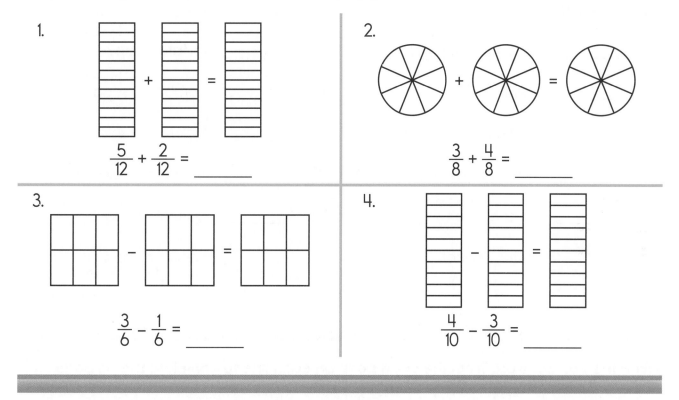

1.

$$\frac{5}{12} + \frac{2}{12} = \underline{\hspace{1cm}}$$

2.

$$\frac{3}{8} + \frac{4}{8} = \underline{\hspace{1cm}}$$

3.

$$\frac{3}{6} - \frac{1}{6} = \underline{\hspace{1cm}}$$

4.

$$\frac{4}{10} - \frac{3}{10} = \underline{\hspace{1cm}}$$

A *relative pronoun* is used to begin a phrase that describes a noun. Some relative pronouns are *that, which,* and *who.* Circle a relative pronoun in each sentence below. Then, write two sentences of your own that use relative pronouns.

5. The twins who live next door are nine years old.

6. My aunt, who lives in California, has invited me to visit during spring break.

7. The DVD that I borrowed from my cousin won't play.

8. Your e-mail, which I received yesterday, was really thoughtful.

9. The hat that you are wearing looks just like the one Dad lost.

10. The birds that nested in the fern have finally laid eggs.

11. _____

12. _____

DAY 18

Read each pair of words. If they are synonyms, write *S* on the line. If they are antonyms, write *A*.

13. _____ ancient modern

14. _____ assist help

15. _____ increase decrease

16. _____ enlarge magnify

17. _____ accept refuse

18. _____ bitter sweet

19. _____ imitate copy

20. _____ combine separate

21. _____ lucky fortunate

22. _____ frequent seldom

23. _____ patient impatient

24. _____ genuine real

Write the correct word from the word bank on each line to complete the passage.

| plant | heat | sunlight | Earth | oxygen | plants |

Sunlight is very important to our planet, _____.

Most of our food comes from _____life.

_____ also give off the _____ we breathe. Without

_____, plants would die, and we would not have

food or air. The _____ of the sun also warms Earth.

Without it, we would freeze.

FACTOID: It took American pioneers from four to six months to travel the 2,000-mile (3,200-kilometer) Oregon Trail.

PLACE STICKER HERE

Solve each problem.

1. 2)224

2. 16
   × 7

3. 3)63

4. 3)156

5. 46
   −28

6. 38
   +17

7. 83
   −47

8. 57
   +34

9. 18
   × 4

10. 24
    × 7

11. 2)256

12. 7)770

13. 804
    −238

14. 132
    − 78

15. 176
    +394

Homophones are words that sound the same but have different meanings and are spelled differently. Write the correct homophone from the parentheses to complete each sentence.

16. I have _____ more days of school. (to, two)

17. Have you_____ this book before? (read, red)

18. That lion has large_____ . (paws, pause)

19. I like that song _____. (two, too)

20. The boys had _____ much work to do before dark. (too, to)

21. _____ is my favorite color. (Red, Read)

22. We are going_____Lake Louise this summer. (to, two)

DAY 19

Add to find each sum. Write each answer in its simplest form.

23. $\frac{1}{3} + \frac{2}{3} =$

24. $\frac{4}{6} + \frac{5}{6} =$

25. $\frac{1}{6} + \frac{1}{6} =$

26. $\frac{3}{6} + \frac{1}{6} =$

27. $\frac{2}{4} + \frac{2}{4} =$

28. $\frac{1}{2} + \frac{1}{2} =$

29. $\frac{5}{8} + \frac{3}{8} =$

30. $\frac{5}{5} + \frac{2}{5} =$

31. $\frac{2}{10} + \frac{4}{10} =$

Write each word from the word bank under the correct heading.

| buttermilk | snowstorm | replanted | peaceful | daylight |
| airplane | selection | sleepless | football | unpacked |

Compound Words

_____

_____

_____

_____

_____

Words with Prefixes or Suffixes

_____

_____

_____

_____

_____

FITNESS FLASH: Do 10 squats.

* See page ii.

PLACE STICKER HERE

Read the passage. Then, answer the questions.

Flash Floods

Rain is good for people and plants. When it rains too much, though, people could be in danger. A flash flood occurs when a lot of rain falls quickly, filling the streets faster than the water can drain. Driving is very dangerous in a flash flood. A person's car could be swept away. If you live in an area where flash flooding is likely, you should listen to radio or TV news reports when it starts to rain. Be ready to leave your home with your family if a newscaster says to move to higher ground. If you leave on foot, do not walk through moving water. Your parents should not drive through standing water unless it is less than 6 inches (15.24 cm) deep. After a flood, listen to news reports. A newscaster will tell you when you can return home safely and when the water from your tap will be safe to drink.

1. What is the main idea of this passage?
   A. Flash floods can be dangerous and occur suddenly.
   B. Never drive through a flooded area.
   C. Take important items with you when you leave your home.

2. What happens during a flash flood? _____

   _____

3. What could happen to a car in a flash flood?_____

   _____

4. What should you do when it starts to rain? _____

   _____

5. How does the author support the idea that flash floods are dangerous to

   people? _____

6. What should you do after a flood? _____

   _____

DAY 20

Solve each equation. Shade the models to help you.

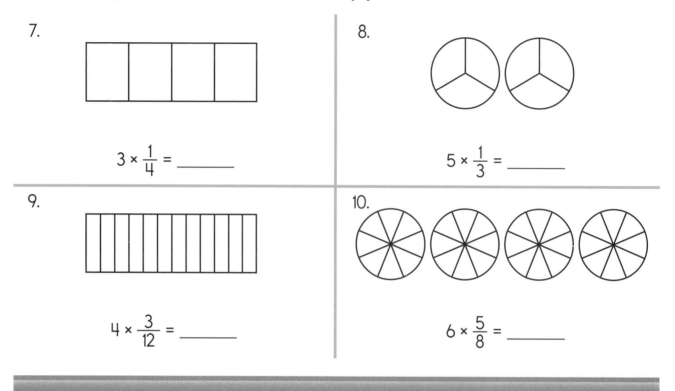

7.

$3 \times \frac{1}{4} =$ _____

8.

$5 \times \frac{1}{3} =$ _____

9.

$4 \times \frac{3}{12} =$ _____

10.

$6 \times \frac{5}{8} =$ _____

Circle each correctly spelled word. Then, write it in the blank to complete each sentence.

11. Astronauts are _____while they are in space.

waitless   weightless   waghtless   wateless

12. The _____ children helped their mother rake leaves.

thotful   toughtful   thoughtful   thowghtful

13. You need to remember to keep your doctor's _____ .

apointment   apowntment   appointment   appointtment

CHARACTER CHECK: What is the golden rule? On a separate sheet of paper, explain the rule using your own words.

PLACE STICKER HERE

Bounce Away!

How much height does a ball lose with each bounce?

Energy is the ability to do work. *Potential energy* is the energy that an object has because of its position. The energy of an object in motion is called *kinetic energy*. If you hold a tennis ball above the ground, it has potential energy due to its position. When the ball is released, gravity pulls it down. The ball's potential energy becomes kinetic energy.

Materials:
- meterstick
- tennis ball

Procedure:

Hold the meterstick vertically with one end against the floor. Hold the tennis ball so that the bottom is at the zero mark.

Drop the ball from a height of 1 meter. Watch carefully to determine the height of the first, second, and third bounces. Round the answer to the nearest centimeter, and record the information on the table below.

Because of the speed at which the ball bounces, you may want to ask another person to help you measure the height of the ball's bounces.

Bounce	Height of Bounce
1	
2	
3	

What's This All About?

The shape of the tennis ball changes slightly when it hits the floor. Some energy is lost as heat (due to friction from air resistance) and when the ball changes shape. Because of the lost energy, the ball will not bounce to the same height it was dropped from. After the ball hits the ground, it returns to its original shape. The energy becomes upward motion as the ball bounces into the air.

Think About It

How are potential and kinetic energy different?

BONUS

Separating Salt and Pepper

How can a mixture of salt and pepper be separated?

Some mixtures are *homogeneous*. This means that they combine evenly. For example, when you mix sugar and water, you get sugar water. The sugar spreads evenly throughout the water.

If you mix sand and water, you get a *heterogeneous* mixture. The sand sinks to the bottom and will not stay mixed with the water.

In this experiment, determine whether salt and pepper is a homogeneous or heterogeneous mixture.

Materials:

- balance or kitchen scale
- pepper
- tray
- balloon
- salt
- your hair (clean and dry)

Procedure:

Use the balance or scale to weigh several teaspoons of salt and pepper. Then, mix the salt and pepper on the tray. Gently shake the tray so that the mixture forms a single layer. Then, blow up the balloon.

Keep your hand in the same place on the balloon and rub the other side of the balloon back and forth about 20 times on your clean, dry hair. Then, hold the balloon about 1 inch (2.5 cm) above the mixture of salt and pepper. The pepper will be attracted to the balloon. Most of the salt will stay where it is.

Pour the remaining mixture onto the balance or scale. Measure the mixture again to find its mass. Record your data on the table.

Trial	Amount of Salt Placed in Mixture	Amount of Salt Remaining in Mixture
1		
2		
3		

Is the mixture of salt and pepper homogeneous or heterogeneous? _____

* See page ii.

Lines of Latitude

Lines of latitude are imaginary lines that run east to west on a map. They are marked in degrees (°) and help people locate places around the world. The equator is the line at 0° latitude. The lines of latitude on the map below are measured in 20° segments from the equator. Places north of the equator have the letter *N* after their degrees. Places south of the equator have the letter *S* after their degrees.

Study the map. Then, answer the questions.

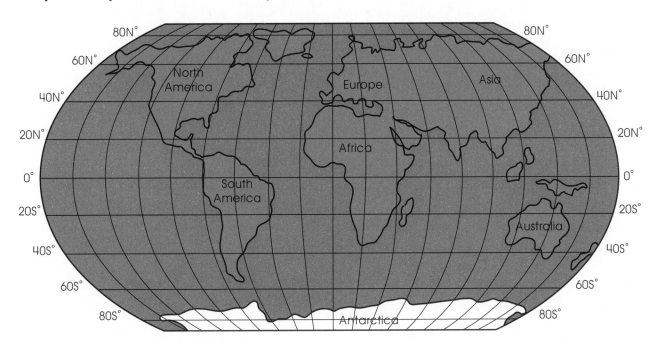

1. The equator is at _____ ° latitude.

2. For locations in North America, the latitude should be followed by the letter_____ .

3. The latitude for the southern tip of South America would be followed

    by the letter _____.

4. Use a red crayon or marker to trace the equator.

BONUS

Latitude and Longitude

Use the map to find the cities located at each latitude and longitude. Then, write the name of each city.

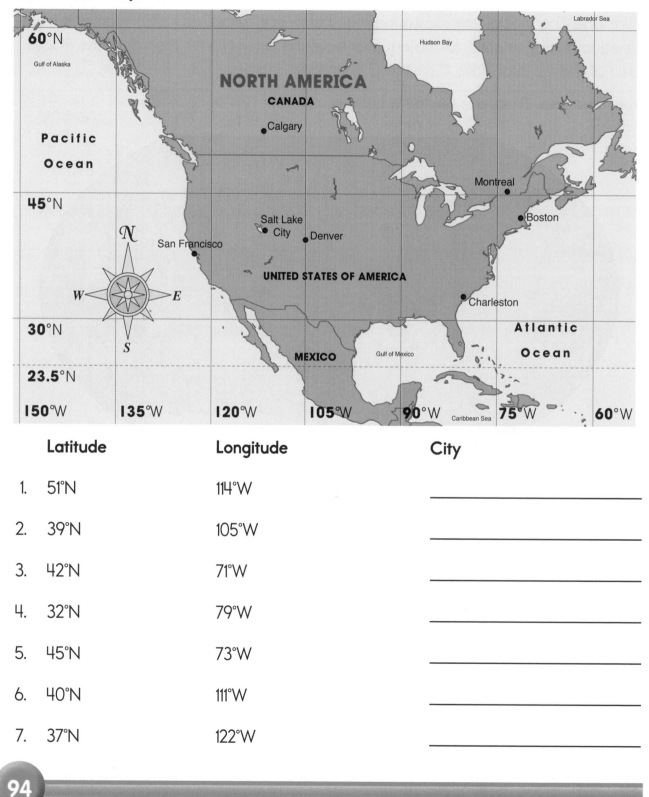

	Latitude	Longitude	City
1.	51°N	114°W	_____
2.	39°N	105°W	_____
3.	42°N	71°W	_____
4.	32°N	79°W	_____
5.	45°N	73°W	_____
6.	40°N	111°W	_____
7.	37°N	122°W	_____

Coat of Arms

A *coat of arms* is a design that belongs to a particular person or family. The colors, symbols, and backgrounds used in a coat of arms all have special meanings and say something about the coat of arms's owner. For example, the color blue may represent truth and loyalty, while a lion may represent courage.

Create a coat of arms. Think of some qualities that you have and are proud of. Brainstorm ways that you could represent those qualities on your coat of arms. Go online with an adult if you need more information. Then, draw your coat of arms in the box.

BONUS

Take It Outside!

Take a tape measure outside four times throughout one day. Each time, have an adult measure the length of your shadow and record the measurements. Then, with an adult, use the computer to search for information about Earth's rotation around the sun. This will help explain why the length of your shadow changes throughout the day.

With an adult, take a thesaurus, a notebook, and a pencil outside. Find a safe, comfortable spot to sit and write the things you see, such as a bird flying, a bee flying, or an airplane flying. Then, find some of the overused words you wrote, such as *flying*. Use a thesaurus to find replacement words that provide better descriptions, such as *soaring*, *gliding*, or *hovering*. Use these new words whenever you can.

How do you find how tall a tree is without a long measuring tape and a tall ladder? You can use the measurements of a tree's shadow and the shadow of a 12-inch ruler to find the height of a tree. First, go outside with an adult and measure the length of a tree's shadow with a measuring tape, yardstick, or meterstick. Then, stand the ruler on its end at a 90° angle from the ground. Use the measuring tape, a yardstick, or a meterstick to find the length of the ruler's shadow. Record the length of each shadow and convert the measurements to the same unit, such as inches. To find the height of the tree, divide the length of the tree's shadow by the length of the ruler's shadow. Then, multiply the answer by the length of the ruler.

For example, if the answer is 10, this means that the tree's shadow is 10 times longer than the ruler, which makes the tree about 10 feet tall.

* See page ii.

Monthly Goals

Think of three goals to set for yourself this month. For example, you may want to exercise for 20 minutes each day. Write your goals on the lines and review them with an adult.

Place a sticker next to each of your goals that you complete. Feel proud that you have met your goals!

1. _____

2. _____

3. _____

Word List

The following words are used in this section. They are good words for you to know. Read each word. Use a dictionary to look up each word that you do not know. Then, write two sentences. Use a word from the word list in each sentence.

central	rely
discuss	rural
interviewing	statue
murmuring	urban
organized	vapor

1. _____

_____

2. _____

_____

Introduction to Endurance

This section includes fitness and character development activities that focus on endurance. These activities are designed to get you moving and thinking about improving your physical fitness and your character. If you have limited mobility, feel free to modify any suggested exercises to fit your individual abilities.

Physical Endurance

What do playing tag, jumping rope, and riding your bike have in common? They are all great ways to build endurance!

Having endurance means doing an activity for a long time before your body becomes tired. Your heart is stronger when you have endurance. Your muscles receive more oxygen.

Use the warm summer mornings and sunny days to go outside. Pick activities that you enjoy. Invite a family member on a walk or a bike ride. Play a game of basketball with friends. Leave the less active times for when it is dark, too hot, or raining.

Set an endurance goal this summer. For example, you might jump rope every day until you can jump for two minutes without stopping. Set new goals when you meet your old ones. Be proud of your endurance success!

Endurance and Character Development

Showing mental endurance means sticking with something. You can show mental endurance every day. Staying with a task when you might want to quit and keeping at it until it is done are ways that you can show mental endurance.

Build your mental endurance this summer. Think of a time when you were frustrated or bored. Maybe you wanted to take swimming lessons. But, after a few early morning lessons, it was not as fun as you imagined. Think about some key points, such as how you asked all spring to take lessons. Be positive. Remind yourself that you have taken only a few lessons. You might get used to the early morning practices. Think of ways to make the lessons more enjoyable, such as sleeping a few extra minutes during the morning car ride. Quitting should be the last option.

Build your mental endurance now. It will help prepare you for challenges you may face later!

Multiply to find each product.

| 1. | 26
× 12 | 2. | 49
× 33 | 3. | 87
× 28 | 4. | 51
× 42 | 5. | 94
× 78 |

| 6. | 81
× 32 | 7. | 23
× 18 | 8. | 55
× 37 | 9. | 62
× 29 | 10. | 75
× 46 |

Read the paragraph. Then, answer the questions.

Sandra's mother offered to help her get ready for the new school year. Sandra grew a full inch taller over the summer. Her shoes were too tight, and her pants were almost above her ankles.

11. What do you think Sandra and her mother will do? _____

_____

_____

12. Which clues helped you decide? _____

_____

_____

FITNESS FLASH: Do 10 jumping jacks.

DAY 1

Complete the table.

	Total Price	Amount Given to Clerk	Change Received
EXAMPLE:	$1.35	$1.50	$0.15
13.	$2.50	$5.00	
14.	$0.95	$1.00	
15.	$1.80	$2.00	
16.	$6.42	$10.00	
17.	$9.35	$20.00	
18.	$5.55	$6.00	
19.	$13.95	$20.00	
20.	$85.00	$100.00	

Underline the correct spelling of each word. If you are unsure, check the spelling in an online or print dictionary.

21. decieve   deceive

22. accompany   acompany

23. exersise   exercise

24. sincerely   sincerley

25. particular   particuler

26. patiunt   patient

27. friend   freind

28. beutiful   beautiful

29. insted   instead

30. becuse   because

31. guard   garde

32. although   althouh

FACTOID: No two snowflakes are exactly alike.

PLACE STICKER HERE

Read the passage. Then, answer the questions.

Food Webs

A *food web* is a drawing that shows how different living things are connected. In a food web, the living things at the bottom are eaten by the animals directly above them. For example, a food web might start at the bottom with plants. Plants do not eat other living things. Above these plants might be small animals, such as mice, that eat plants. Larger animals, such as owls and snakes, eat mice. A food web can tell us what might happen if certain plants or animals disappear from an **ecosystem**, or the surroundings in which all of the plants and animals live. In the food web described above, if something happened to the plants, then the mice would not have as much food. This would affect the owls and snakes, who would also not have enough food. Soon, there would be fewer of each type of animal. This is why it is important to protect all living things in an ecosystem, not just the larger ones.

1. What is the main idea of this passage?
    A. Food webs show how all living things are connected.
    B. Owls and snakes are the most important animals.
    C. Only the animals at the top of the food web should be protected.

2. What is a food web? _____

    _____

3. What is an ecosystem?
    A. a food web for very large animals
    B. the surroundings where a group of plants and animals live
    C. a place where only plants grow

4. How does the author support the idea that it is important to protect all living

    things in an ecosystem?_____

    _____

    _____

DAY 2

Find each equivalent measurement.

2 cups = 1 pint	4 quarts = 1 gallon
2 pints = 1 quart	16 cups = 1 gallon

5. 5 quarts = _____ pints

6. 3 gallons = _____ pints

7. 4 cups = _____ pints

8. 2 pints = _____ cups

9. _____ gallons = 16 pints

10. 5 gallons = _____ quarts

11. _____ pints = 2 quarts

12. 3 quarts = _____ cups

Double the Fun (and Falls)

Boost your endurance and help a friend or family member get fit, too. Make an outdoor obstacle course using soft objects, such as piles of leaves, to run around and hop over. Mark a turnaround spot so that you can retrace your hops and repeat the course. Use two strong, soft pieces of fabric to tie yourself to your partner above the ankles and knees. Remember that you must work together to complete this course. For the first time through, walk the route and discuss your strategy. For the following turn, time your performance. Then, set a goal and repeat the course to try to beat your time. Encourage each other to challenge yourselves. Keep going until you reach your goal!

 **FITNESS FLASH: Jog in place for 30 seconds.**

* See page ii.

PLACE STICKER HERE

Do you think schools should schedule two recesses each day? Why or why not? Support your opinion with facts and reasons and include a conclusion.

_____

_____

_____

_____

_____

Read each sentence. Write *F* if it is a fact. Write *O* if it is an opinion.

EXAMPLE:

_____**F**_____ Abraham Lincoln was the 16th president of the United States.

1. _____ Spring is the best time of the year.

2. _____ Chocolate cake is the best dessert in the world.

3. _____ Daytime and nighttime depend on the position of the sun in the sky.

4. _____ Dogs are the best pets.

5. _____ Neil Armstrong walked on the moon in 1969.

6. _____ Lava rock was once hot liquid.

7. _____ Eating too much candy is bad for your teeth.

8. _____ Everyone should like chocolate ice cream.

9. _____ Reading is the best way to spend a rainy day.

DAY 3

Read the passage. Then, answer the questions.

Edward Murrow

Edward Murrow was an American journalist. He became famous during World War II. Murrow was born in 1908 in North Carolina. After college, he began working for a radio station. Many Americans listened to his live broadcasts during the bombing of London, England, in September 1939. Before Murrow's reports, people in the United States learned about the war through newsreels in movie theaters or articles in newspapers. Now, they could learn about the war in London as it was happening. After the war, Murrow worked as a reporter in radio, then in television. He became known for interviewing, or asking questions of, important people. Other newscasters followed in Murrow's footsteps. Today, we still rely on reporters in other countries for news and information. And, we still listen to reporters' conversations with famous people.

10. What is the main idea of this passage?
    A. Edward Murrow was a brave American journalist.
    B. Edward Murrow talked to many famous people.
    C. Edward Murrow worked in London.

11. What type of company did Murrow work for after college?

    _____

12. How did people learn about the war before Murrow's reports?

    _____

13. Write a brief summary of the passage._____

    _____

14. How did Murrow change the way journalists work? _____

    _____

> **FACTOID: Giant squids have the largest eyes of any creature on Earth.**

PLACE
STICKER
HERE

Write factor pairs for each number.

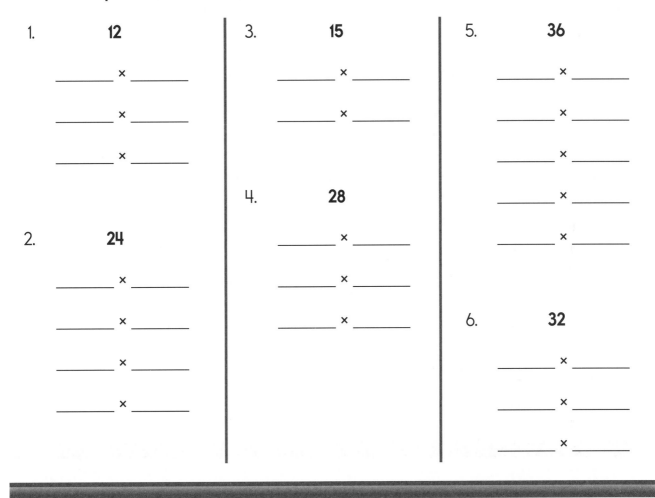

1.   **12**

_____ × _____

_____ × _____

_____ × _____

2.   **24**

_____ × _____

_____ × _____

_____ × _____

_____ × _____

3.   **15**

_____ × _____

_____ × _____

4.   **28**

_____ × _____

_____ × _____

_____ × _____

5.   **36**

_____ × _____

_____ × _____

_____ × _____

_____ × _____

_____ × _____

6.   **32**

_____ × _____

_____ × _____

_____ × _____

Complete each sentence by writing *more than*, *less than*, or *equal to*.

| 2 cups = 1 pint | 2 pints = 1 quart | 4 quarts = 1 gallon |

7.   2 pints are _____ 1 quart.

8.   1 gallon is _____ 1 pint.

9.   1 pint is _____ 1 quart.

10.   6 pints are _____ 3 quarts.

11.   3 quarts are _____ 1 gallon.

12.   2 pints are _____ 4 cups.

13.   3 cups are _____ 1 quart.

14.   8 quarts are _____ 2 gallons.

DAY 4

Sometimes formal language is needed, and sometimes informal language is appropriate. Read each pair of sentences. Write *I* next to sentences with informal language, and *F* next to those with formal language.

15. _____ Earth is home to approximately 4,000 types of cockroaches.

_____ This is totally unbelievable, but there are about 4,000 different kinds of cockroaches!

16. _____ See ya later!

_____ I look forward to seeing you again soon.

17. _____ You've gotta see this ginormous, awesome pumpkin Peter grew in his garden.

_____ You must see the large, impressive pumpkin Peter grew in his garden.

18. _____ It's been a pleasure to speak with you.

_____ Nice talking to you.

Continue each counting pattern.

19.   0   3   6   9   12   ____   ____   ____   24   ____

20.   6   12   18   24   ____   ____   ____   48   ____   ____

21.   12   16   20   24   ____   ____   ____   ____   44   ____

22.   33   30   27   24   ____   ____   ____   ____   9   ____

23.   100   98   96   94   ____   ____   ____   86   ____   ____

Read the story. Then, answer the questions.

Ivy's grandmother will celebrate her 70th birthday soon. Ivy wants to get her grandmother a special gift, but she spent her money on new books instead. Ivy loves reading about Mexico. Her grandmother came from Mexico, and she read to Ivy when Ivy was little. Lately, her grandmother's eyesight has been failing, so she can no longer see the words on the page.

1. What do you think Ivy will do?_____

_____

2. Which clues helped you decide? _____

_____

Fractions that have a denominator of 10 can also be written as decimals. Write each fraction and/or decimal.

EXAMPLE:

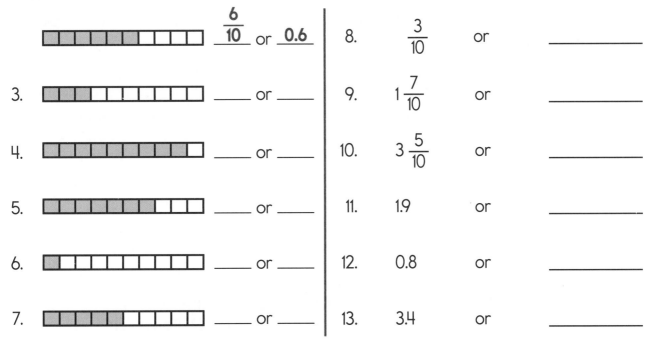

$\frac{6}{10}$ or **0.6**

3. ____ or ____

4. ____ or ____

5. ____ or ____

6. ____ or ____

7. ____ or ____

8. $\frac{3}{10}$ or _____

9. $1\frac{7}{10}$ or _____

10. $3\frac{5}{10}$ or _____

11. 1.9 or _____

12. 0.8 or _____

13. 3.4 or _____

DAY 5

Read each set of adjectives in parentheses ( ). Decide what order they should be in to describe the object. Rewrite the words in that order, as shown in the example.

EXAMPLE: hat (black large fuzzy) _____large fuzzy black hat_____

14.   bottles (empty six water) _____

15.   box (cardboard musty brown) _____

16.   teacup (pink small) _____

17.   sweater (gray wool cozy) _____

18.   trucks (three yellow plastic large) _____

19.   salad (Greek fresh small) _____

20.   snake (brown poisonous) _____

Fit Tag

Get fit with this version of freeze tag! Invite several friends or family members to play. Start by choosing someone to be "it." That person must chase and tag everyone until all of the players are "frozen." Frozen players perform an ongoing exercise, such as jumping jacks or running in place. Players who are free can unfreeze their teammates by tapping them on their shoulders. The last person frozen becomes "it." Continue playing until everyone has gotten a good endurance-boosting workout.

> **CHARACTER CHECK:** "When you get to the end of your rope, tie a knot and hang on." Franklin D. Roosevelt

* See page ii.

PLACE STICKER HERE

Read the story. Then, write the meaning of each word.

Gabe lives in a large city with his grandparents. The building that he and his grandparents live in is very tall and has different sets of rooms for each family that lives there. This building is called an apartment building. In this community, all of the buildings are close together. People do not have to go far to get things they need in this urban area. Gabe's cousin, Jasper, lives in a rural, or country, community. He plays in his large backyard instead of in a park like Gabe. There is a lot of space between houses where Jasper lives. Both Gabe's and Jasper's neighborhoods have schools, hospitals, and stores.

1. community _____

_____

2. urban _____

_____

3. rural _____

_____

Subtract to find each difference. Write answers in simplest form.

EXAMPLE:
$\dfrac{4}{5} - \dfrac{1}{5} = \dfrac{3}{5}$ ◄——— subtract the numerators
◄——— keep the same denominator

4. $\dfrac{2}{6} - \dfrac{1}{6} =$

5. $\dfrac{5}{10} - \dfrac{3}{10} =$

6. $\dfrac{3}{4} - \dfrac{2}{4} =$

7. $6\dfrac{8}{10}$
    $-\ 3\dfrac{4}{10}$

8. $8\dfrac{4}{10}$
    $-\ 3\dfrac{3}{10}$

9. $7\dfrac{2}{15}$
    $-\ 3\dfrac{1}{15}$

DAY 6

Read the journal entries and answer the questions that follow.

July 14, 1935

I am almost too tired tonight to write. The days seem to stretch on forever. Before dawn, we're up to do the milking. I make mush for breakfast nearly every day. We are weary of mush, though I know I should be grateful to have it.

We grow most of our own food, but the harvests are hard work. I wish we had more help, but we can barely pay the hired hands we already have.

President Roosevelt says this Depression will not last forever. Is he right? The most important thing is that we do not lose this farm. "You worry too much for a girl your age, Elizabeth," says Mama. It is hard not to worry in these times.

August 8, 1935

We are so lucky to live in a place where people have such generous spirits. Del Landon from up the road helped Sam fix the holes in the fence. Mrs. Carson brought us fruit preserves and a bag of outgrown clothes.

The best news of all is that we'll have help with our harvest. "Many hands make light work," Pa says, and he's right. When it's time for their crops to come in, we'll help our neighbors, too. Folks need to rely on each other. We'll make it through. I know we will. Better times must be ahead.

10. Write a brief summary of the passage. _____

_____

11. Tell what you know about Elizabeth's character, based on her journal entries.

_____

12. What does the saying "Many hands make light work" mean? _____

13. From what point of view is this story told? How does the point of view add to the

story? _____

PLACE
STICKER
HERE

Find each equivalent measurement.

1. 15 meters = _____ centimeters

2. 6,000 meters = _____ kilometers

3. _____ centimeters = 250 millimeters

4. 1 meter = _____ millimeters

5. 85 meters = _____ centimeters

6. _____ kilometers = 500 meters

7. 3,000 millimeters = _____ meters

8. 15,000 meters = _____ kilometers

> 1 centimeter = 10 millimeters
> 1 meter = 100 centimeters
> 1 kilometer = 1,000 meters

In each sentence, underline the cause and circle the effect.

EXAMPLE: The sky became cloudy, then it started to snow.

9. The cold weather caused frost to cover the windows.

10. The falling snowflakes made my cheeks wet and cold.

11. Snow stuck to my mittens because I had made a snowman.

12. The snowman melted from the heat of the sun.

13. I swam so long in the pool that I had to put on more sunscreen.

14. Cayce missed the bus because she overslept.

15. Because Shay watched a scary movie on TV, she could not fall asleep.

16. The lady was thirsty, so she went to get a glass of water.

DAY 7

Imagine that a famous person has come to visit you at home. Who is it? What do you talk about? What is he or she like? Write a narrative that tells about your experience with this person. Be sure to use descriptive details. Include some dialogue in your writing.

_____

_____

_____

_____

_____

Compare the decimal numbers. Use the greater than (>), less than (<), or equal to (=) symbols.

17. 0.25 ◯ 2.50

18. 0.09 ◯ 0.19

19. 1.50 ◯ 1.05

20. 0.45 ◯ 0.5

21. 3.3 ◯ 0.33

22. 0.52 ◯ 0.05

23. 1.10 ◯ 0.11

24. 0.79 ◯ 0.8

25. 0.45 ◯ 4.50

26. 0.20 ◯ 0.2

27. 5.87 ◯ 7.58

28. 0.45 ◯ 0.54

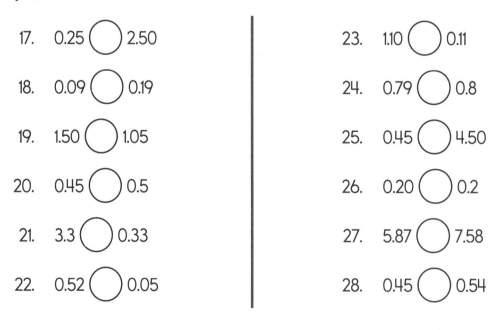

FITNESS FLASH: Hop on your right foot for 30 seconds.

* See page ii.

PLACE STICKER HERE

Read the passage. Then, answer the questions.

Planning a City

What do the streets in your city look like? Some cities have streets that are very straight and organized. It is easy to get from one point in the city to another. Other cities have streets that seem to go nowhere. It may be difficult to give directions to your home.

In the past, when a group of people moved to a place and started planning the streets, some of them used something called a *grid system*. One example of this is found in the city of Philadelphia, Pennsylvania, which is divided into four sections around a central square. The map was laid out by William Penn in 1682. The grid included wide streets that were easy for people to walk down. Penn left London, England, after a fire destroyed most of the city. London had a maze of narrow streets that were hard to move around safely. Penn wanted to make sure that people could get around easily and safely. Many other people followed Penn's ideas when setting up their new cities' street systems.

1. What is the main idea of this passage?
    A. William Penn drew the first grid system.
    B. Planning a city is important for safety and ease of use.
    C. Some streets are straight and organized.

2. What is one good thing about having straight streets? _____

    _____

3. What is a grid system?
    A. a plan for developing a city's streets
    B. an area of the classroom
    C. a TV channel

4. When did Penn leave London? _____

    _____

5. How are Philadelphia's streets different from London's? _____

    _____

DAY 8

A figure is symmetrical if it can be folded in half so that the two parts are congruent. Draw one line of symmetry for each figure.

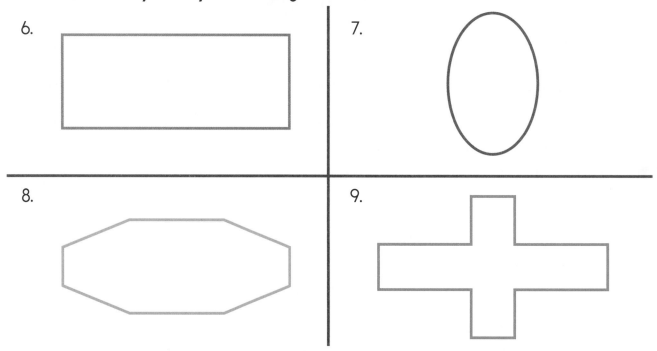

6.

7.

8.

9.

Unscramble the words in parentheses to complete each analogy.

10. Pillows are to soft as boards are to _____. (rdha)

11. Bells are to ring as car horns are to _____. (nkho)

12. Hear is to ears as touch is to _____. (serinfg)

13. Star is to pointed as circle is to _____ . (dunor)

14. Fish is to swim as bird is to _____ . (ylf)

15. Elephant is to large as mouse is to _____. (malsl)

16. Paint is to brush as draw is to _____. (cienlp)

FACTOID: A sneeze can travel at a speed of more than 100 miles (160.9 km) per hour.

PLACE STICKER HERE

Use the table to answer each question.

Student Music Lesson Schedule

Day 1 (new students only)	Day 2	Day 3	Day 4	Day 5
Nicole	José	Solina	Greg	Jamie
Naomi	Kira	Jamie	Kipley	Solina
Tanya	Kipley	Greg	Jacob	Rebecca
Michelle	Mark	Rebecca	José	Mark
Fiora	Jacob	Margaret	Kira	Drake

1. Other than Jacob, who has a lesson on day 4? _____

   _____

2. Tanya, Naomi, and Fiora all have a lesson on which day? _____

3. How many lessons is Jacob scheduled for in all? _____

4. Kipley, Naomi, and Mark practice together. Who is the new music student?

   _____

5. How many new students are there altogether? _____

6. Why does Mark not have a lesson on day 1? _____

   _____

If you could be any animal, which animal would you be? Why?

_____

_____

_____

DAY 9

Does the dotted line in each figure represent a line of symmetry? Circle *yes* or *no*.

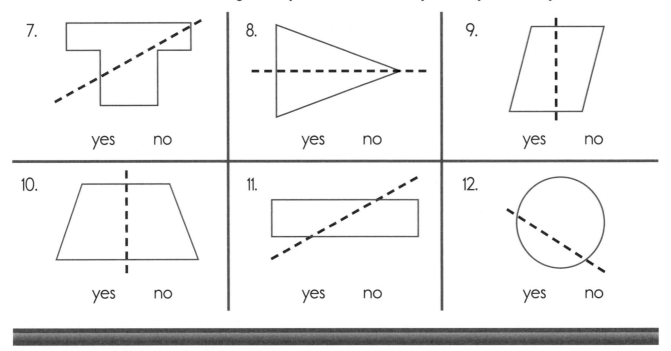

7.   yes   no

8.   yes   no

9.   yes   no

10.   yes   no

11.   yes   no

12.   yes   no

Use the progressive verb tense (a form of *be* + main verb + *ing*) to answer each question below.

EXAMPLE: What are the puppies doing right now?
The puppies **are playing** in the backyard.

13.   What will you be doing at noon tomorrow?

_____

14.   What are you working on right now?

_____

15.   What were you doing at this time yesterday?

_____

16.   What will you eat for dinner tomorrow?

_____

PLACE
STICKER
HERE

Read the passage and answer the questions that follow.

King Midas

One day, King Midas was strolling through his garden. He came across the teacher Silenus, who had taken ill. Midas nursed the old man back to health. The Greek god Dionysus was joyful at the return of his beloved friend Silenus. He allowed the king to make one wish, though he warned him to choose wisely.

King Midas decided quickly. "I would like to have everything I touch turn to gold," he said. Dionysus found the king to be very foolish. Still, he granted the wish.

King Midas grabbed a twig from a tree. His fingers touched the branch, and it immediately turned to gold. *Amazing!* thought the king. Once he returned home, he ran from room to room, turning things to gold. A golden chair! Golden flowers! A golden staircase!

When the king sat down to feast that night, he reached for a loaf of bread. It turned to gold in his hands. He tried to spoon vegetables onto his plate and sip from his cup of water, but they too turned to gold. The king's daughter entered the room at that moment. She saw the look of worry on her father's face and rushed to hug him. He did not have time to warn her away, and the beautiful young girl turned into a statue of gold.

1. Why does Dionysus offer to grant a wish for the king?_____

2. Why does Dionysus find the king to be foolish?_____

    _____

3. What lesson does this myth teach? What other genre of writing often has a

    moral or lesson? _____

    _____

4. What do you think will happen next in the story?_____

    _____

DAY 10

Add to find each sum. Before adding, you may need to change the denominator of one fraction from 10 to 100. Remember to multiply both the numerator and denominator by 10.

EXAMPLE: $\frac{1}{10} + \frac{15}{100} = \frac{25}{100}$

(Think: $\frac{10}{100} + \frac{15}{100} = \frac{25}{100}$.)

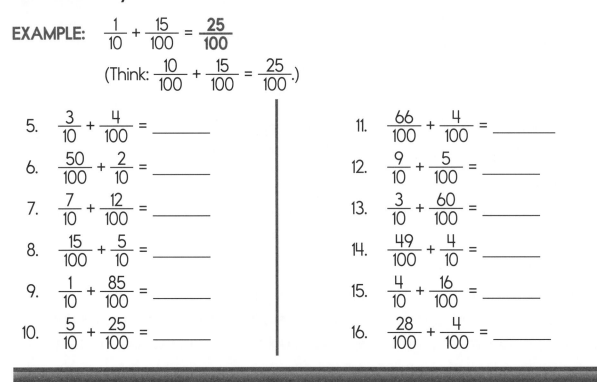

5. $\frac{3}{10} + \frac{4}{100} = $ _____

6. $\frac{50}{100} + \frac{2}{10} = $ _____

7. $\frac{7}{10} + \frac{12}{100} = $ _____

8. $\frac{15}{100} + \frac{5}{10} = $ _____

9. $\frac{1}{10} + \frac{85}{100} = $ _____

10. $\frac{5}{10} + \frac{25}{100} = $ _____

11. $\frac{66}{100} + \frac{4}{100} = $ _____

12. $\frac{9}{10} + \frac{5}{100} = $ _____

13. $\frac{3}{10} + \frac{60}{100} = $ _____

14. $\frac{49}{100} + \frac{4}{10} = $ _____

15. $\frac{4}{10} + \frac{16}{100} = $ _____

16. $\frac{28}{100} + \frac{4}{100} = $ _____

Write about your experience of learning how to do something new. Who helped you? What did you learn? Share your story using a logical sequence of events.

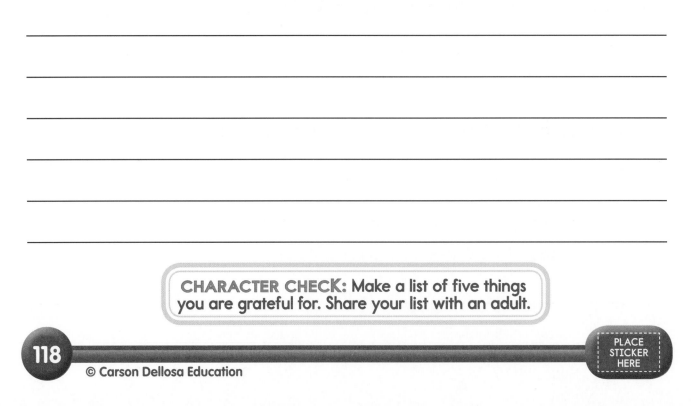

_____

_____

_____

_____

_____

_____

CHARACTER CHECK: Make a list of five things you are grateful for. Share your list with an adult.

PLACE STICKER HERE

Look at each underlined idiom. Then, choose the correct meaning of each sentence.

1. Cody was <u>back to square one</u> when his dog chewed his science fair project.
    A. Cody stood on a square that was labeled *one*.
    B. Cody had to start his science fair project again from the beginning.
    C. Cody was unhappy that his dog chewed up his science fair project.

2. <u>Time flies</u> when we are having fun.
    A. Time seems to go quickly when we are having fun.
    B. Time has wings and flies like a bird.
    C. Time goes slowly.

3. Torika needs to <u>toe the line</u> if she wants to go to the movies.
    A. Torika needs to behave if she wants to go to the movies.
    B. Torika needs to stand behind a line if she wants to go to the movies.
    C. Torika needs to stand in line for a movie ticket.

The Power of Perseverance

The word *perseverance* means to keep going even if something is difficult. Think of someone you know whom you admire or consider a hero, like a grandparent. Ask this person if you can conduct an interview. Ask your hero questions to try to determine what made him successful. What struggles did he overcome? What made him persevere? Write the answers to those questions. After interviewing your hero, write a key quote from him that explains his perseverance, such as, "I always tried my best because I wanted to be my best." Post the quote where you can see it every day as a reminder to never give up.

DAY 11

Subtract to find each difference. Regroup if needed.

4. $7.36
   −$3.97

5. $8.90
   −$2.49

6. $7.68
   −$4.79

7. $3.85
   −$2.79

8. $7.47
   −$4.58

9. $8.37
   −$2.09

10. $4.76
   −$2.67

11. $6.89
   −$4.78

12. $6.77
   −$2.88

13. $3.76
   −$1.87

What is the best thing you did this summer?

_____

_____

_____

_____

_____

_____

_____

_____

_____

FACTOID: A flea can jump 200 times the length of its body.

PLACE
STICKER
HERE

Solve the problems. Write remainders like this: R4.

1. 3)5,422

2. 8)687

3. 9)1,599

4. 4)428

5. 3)755

6. 4)4,624

7. 7)878

8. 2)2,542

9. 5)374

10. 6)954

11. 9)1,000

12. 3)752

Imagine that you are asked to invent a new word. What would the word be, and what would it mean?

_____

_____

_____

_____

DAY 12

Read the passage. Then, answer the questions.

Matter

All matter on Earth exists in one of three states: solid, liquid, or gas. Solids, such as boxes or books, have certain shapes that are difficult to change. Liquids, such as lemonade or orange juice, take the shape of the containers they are in. Gases, such as the air you breathe and helium, spread out to fill the space they are in. It is easy to change water from one state to another. The water you drink is a liquid. When water is heated, such as in a pot on the stove, it becomes a gas. This gas is known as steam, or vapor. Steam can be used in a large machine to make electricity. When water is frozen, such as in a tray in the freezer, it turns to ice. Ice can be used to help a hurt part of the body heal.

13. What is the main idea of this passage?
     A. Steam is heated water.
     B. All matter exists as a solid, a liquid, or a gas.
     C. Ice cubes make water taste better.

14. What are two examples of solids? _____

15. What are two examples of liquids?_____

16. What are two examples of gases? _____

17. Water can exist as a solid, a liquid, or a gas. What is it called in each state?

     _____

18. How are solids, liquids, and gases different from each other?_____

     _____

     _____

     _____

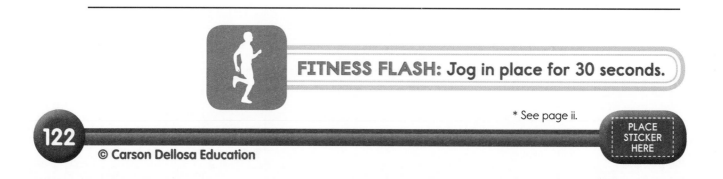

FITNESS FLASH: Jog in place for 30 seconds.

* See page ii.

PLACE STICKER HERE

Add to find each sum. Write each answer in simplest form.

1. $\frac{1}{4} + \frac{3}{4} =$

2. $\frac{3}{5} + \frac{2}{5} =$

3. $\frac{3}{7} + \frac{2}{7} =$

4. $\frac{3}{4} + \frac{1}{4} =$

5. $\frac{1}{7} + \frac{1}{7} =$

6. $\frac{1}{6} + \frac{4}{6} =$

Write the correct homophone from the word bank to complete each sentence.

I	eye	you	ewe	wear	where

7. My friend and _____ ate sandwiches and apples for lunch.

8. The _____ took care of her lamb.

9. Cory got a speck of dust in his _____.

10. Do you know _____ to put the books away?

11. Would _____ please hand me that pencil?

12. Hillary will _____ her blue shoes today.

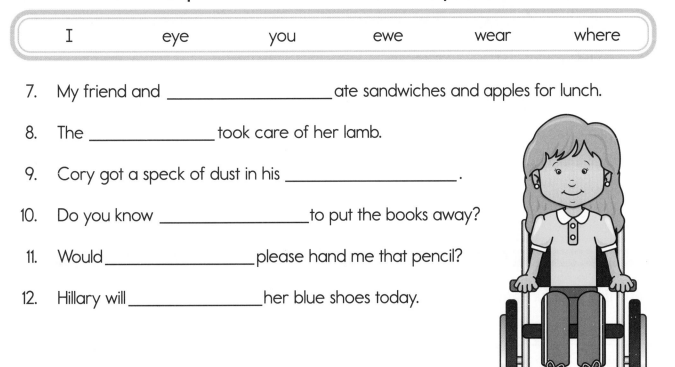

DAY 13

Circle your answer to each question. Then, underline the root.

13. Which word contains a Latin root that means "to see"? Underline the root.

    spectacles   perimeter   automobile

14. Which word contains a Greek root that means "earth"? Underline the root.

    erupt   eject   geology

15. Which word contains a Greek root that means "measure"? Underline the root.

    structure   thermometer   hydrogen

16. Which word contains a Latin root that means "water"? Underline the root.

    automatic   zoology   aquarium

17. Which word contains a Latin root that means "foot"? Underline the root.

    pedal   decade   universe

18. Which word contains a Latin root that means "between"? Underline the root.

    interrupt   attract   telescope

19. Which word contains a Greek root that means "three"? Underline the root.

    quarter   unicycle   triplets

20. Which word contains a Greek root that means "write or draw"? Underline the root.

    century   autograph   stethoscope

Describe your dream vacation. Where would you go? What would you do?

_____

_____

_____

PLACE
STICKER
HERE

Read the passage. Then, answer the questions.

Health and Fitness

Health and fitness are important for you and your family. If you start good health habits now, you will have a better chance of being a healthy adult later. You may go to physical education class several times a week, but you should also try to stay fit outside of school. You and your family can make healthy choices together. You can choose fresh fruit for dessert instead of cake. Offer to help make dinner one night, and surprise your family by preparing a delicious salad. You can go for a walk together after dinner instead of watching TV. Exercising can help wake up your brain so that you can do a good job on your homework. Making healthy choices may seem hard now, but it will feel good after a while.

1. What is the main idea of this passage?
   A. Going to physical education class is fun.
   B. Making healthy choices is too hard.
   C. Health and fitness are important for you and your family.

2. What might happen if you start good health habits now? _____

   _____

3. How does the author support the idea that good health is important? _____

   _____

4. What is a better choice than cake for dessert? _____

5. What can you do instead of watching TV after dinner? _____

   _____

6. Find another source of information about health and fitness. You can go online with an adult's help or look for a book at the library. On a separate sheet of paper, write a paragraph that summarizes what you have learned about health and fitness.

DAY 14

Solve each word problem. Show your work.

7. Isaiah had 2 hours of free time. He spent $\frac{1}{4}$ of an hour eating a snack, $\frac{1}{4}$ of an hour talking with his brother, and $1\frac{1}{4}$ hours reading. How much time did he have left?

8. Hanna walked $\frac{1}{3}$ mile to the store, $\frac{2}{3}$ mile to the library, and $\frac{1}{3}$ mile home. How far did she walk in all?

9. A grocery clerk placed $\frac{5}{8}$ pound of butter, $\frac{1}{8}$ pound of raisins, $\frac{3}{8}$ pound of lettuce, and 2 pounds of potatoes into a bag. What was the total weight of the items?

10. Eddy had a piece of cloth. He used $\frac{5}{16}$ of the cloth for a bandana and gave $\frac{9}{16}$ of the cloth to his sister. How much of the cloth is left?

Circle each word that needs a capital letter.

4407 ninth street
hillside, maine 04024

march 10, 2014

skateboards and more
6243 rock avenue
detroit, michigan 48201

To whom it may concern:

I am returning my skateboard for repair. it is still under warranty. please repair it and return the skateboard to the address above as soon as possible.

sincerely,

wesley diaz

FITNESS FLASH: Hop on your left foot 10 times.

* See page ii.

PLACE STICKER HERE

Solve the problems.

1. 5,422
    × 3

2. 9,260
    × 5

3. 285
    × 4

4. 3,164
    × 8

5. 907
    × 6

6. 8,616
    × 7

7. 6,182
    × 9

8. 5,481
    × 2

Separate each run-on sentence into two sentences. Use correct capitalization and punctuation to write the new sentences.

9. Raven has a new backpack it is green and has many zippers.

    _____

10. Katie borrowed my pencil she plans to draw a map.

    _____

11. Zoe is outside she is on the swings.

    _____

12. Zack is helping Dad Elroy is helping Dad too.

    _____

DAY 15

Read the passage. Then, answer the questions.

Snowflakes
by Mary Mapes Dodge

Whenever a snowflake leaves the sky,
It turns and turns to say "Good-by!
Good-by, dear clouds, so cool and gray!"
Then lightly travels on its way.

And when a snowflake finds a tree,
"Good-day!" it says—"Good-day to thee!
Thou art so bare and lonely, dear,
I'll rest and call my comrades here."

But when a snowflake, brave and meek,
Lights on a rosy maiden's cheek,
It starts—"How warm and soft the day!
'Tis summer!"—and it melts away.

13. Which pattern describes the poem's rhyme scheme?
    A.   ABC ABC
    B.   AA BB
    C.   AB AB

14. What does the author personify in this poem? _____

15. What are the different sections of a poem called?
    A.   paragraphs
    B.   rhythms
    C.   stanzas

16. According to the poem, when does the snowflake think it's summer? _____

_____

CHARACTER CHECK: Think of three things that you like about yourself. Write these characteristics on a separate sheet of paper, and post it where you will see it often.

PLACE
STICKER
HERE

Read the story. Then, answer the questions.

Julie and Clint closed their eyes to shut out the sun's glare. As they sat on the ground, the hot July sun felt good. They could hear the wind blowing softly through the pine trees, making a kind of whispering, murmuring sound. They could hear the creek nearby making soothing, babbling sounds. They could even hear the distant screech of a hawk flying high in the sky overhead.

1. Where do you think Julie and Clint are? _____

2. What season of the year is it? _____

3. What could Julie and Clint hear? _____

_____

4. What would you like to do if you were there? _____

_____

Imagine that you are having a party to celebrate something good. Write about what you are celebrating. Then, on a separate sheet of paper, design an invitation for your party.

_____

_____

_____

_____

_____

_____

DAY 16

Add to find each sum. Regroup if needed.

5.
```
  246
+ 129
```

6.
```
  500
+ 806
```

7.
```
  924
+ 289
```

8.
```
  402
+ 629
```

9.
```
  1,284
+ 2,629
```

10.
```
  7,762
+ 1,473
```

11.
```
  3,383
+ 5,007
```

12.
```
  4,290
+ 2,968
```

13.
```
  9,542
+   695
```

14.
```
  2,423
+ 1,932
```

Use the place value chart to write each number or number word.

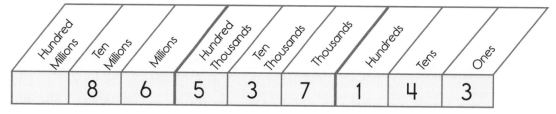

Hundred Millions	Ten Millions	Millions	Hundred Thousands	Ten Thousands	Thousands	Hundreds	Tens	Ones
	8	6	5	3	7	1	4	3

EXAMPLE:

Eighty-six million five hundred thirty-seven thousand one hundred forty-three

<u>   **86,537,143**   </u>

15. One million three hundred sixty-nine thousand _____

16. Five hundred two million one hundred thousand seven _____

17. 375,403,101 _____

_____

18. 894,336,045 _____

_____

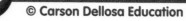

PLACE STICKER HERE

Subtract to find each difference. Regroup if needed.

1. 3.01
    −2.42

2. 5.41
    −3.77

3. 4.71
    −3.82

4. 7.27
    −4.19

5. 8.48
    −3.99

6. 8.47
    −3.58

7. 5.02
    −3.21

8. 7.04
    −6.67

9. 8.46
    −4.57

10. 6.03
    −2.77

Read the story. Then, answer the questions.

Swimming Lessons

Ann and her brother took swimming lessons this summer. Because they live in the country, they took a bus to the pool. It took half an hour to get there. Their lessons were two hours long, then they rode the bus home. Even though it took a lot of time, they enjoyed it very much. By the end of the summer, they both knew how to swim well.

11. What is the best summary for this story?
    A. Ann and her brother took swimming lessons this summer.
    B. Ann and her brother rode a bus to the pool to take swimming lessons this summer. They enjoyed it and both learned how to swim.

12. Should a summary be longer or shorter than the original story? _____

13. What information should be included in the summary? _____

_____

_____

_____

DAY 17

Rewrite each fraction as a decimal.

14. $\dfrac{15}{100}$ = _____

15. $\dfrac{7}{10}$ = _____

16. $\dfrac{58}{100}$ = _____

17. $\dfrac{9}{100}$ = _____

18. $\dfrac{60}{100}$ = _____

19. $\dfrac{6}{10}$ = _____

20. $\dfrac{81}{100}$ = _____

21. $\dfrac{32}{100}$ = _____

22. $\dfrac{5}{100}$ = _____

23. $\dfrac{5}{10}$ = _____

24. $\dfrac{55}{100}$ = _____

25. $\dfrac{3}{10}$ = _____

Read each group of words. Write *S* if it is a sentence, *F* if it is a fragment, or *R* if it is a run-on sentence.

26. _____ Orangutans are rare animals.

27. _____ Live in rain forests in Borneo and Sumatra.

28. _____ They belong to the ape family along with the chimpanzees and gorillas they are larger than most chimpanzees and smaller than most gorillas.

29. _____ Approximately three to five feet tall.

30. _____ Their arms are extremely long.

FITNESS FLASH: Hop on your left foot for 30 seconds.

* See page ii.

PLACE STICKER HERE

Where would you find the answer to each of the following questions? Write the name of the best reference from the word bank.

| globe | dictionary | encyclopedia |

1. Where is Oregon? _____

2. How do they harvest sugarcane in Hawaii? _____

3. Which syllable is stressed in the word *Utah*? _____

4. What kind of food do people eat in Mexico? _____

5. Which continent is closest to Australia? _____

6. Where is the Indian Ocean? _____

7. Who was Thomas Edison, and what did he do? _____

8. What does the word *hibernate* mean? _____

9. What are two different meanings for the word *project*? _____

The proofreading mark ʌ is used to show where a word, letter, or punctuation mark needs to be added in a sentence. Use the proofreading mark ʌ to show where commas are needed in each sentence.

10. As a bird of prey the American kestrel eats insects mice lizards and other birds.

11. Birds of prey such as hawks have hooked beaks and feet with claws.

12. Falcons are powerful fliers and they can swoop from great heights.

13. The American kestrel the smallest North American falcon is only 8 inches (20.3 cm) long.

14. "Kim let's look at this book about falcons."

Read the passage. Then, answer the questions.

Scientific Experiments

Scientists learn about the world by conducting experiments. They take careful notes about the supplies they use and the results they find. They share their findings with others, which leads to everyone learning a little more. You can do experiments, too! The library has many books with safe experiments for students. You might work with balloons, water, or baking soda. You might learn about how light travels or why marbles roll down a ramp. Ask an adult to help you set up your experiment and to make sure that you are being safe. Be sure to wash your hands afterward and clean up the area. Take good notes about your work. Remember, you may be able to change just one thing the next time to get a completely different result. Most of all, do not worry if your results are different from what you expected. Some of the greatest scientific discoveries were made by mistake!

15. What is the main idea of this passage?
    A. Scientists learn about the world by conducting experiments.
    B. Scientists sometimes make mistakes that lead to great discoveries.
    C. You should always take good notes when conducting an experiment.

16. What do scientists take notes about? _____

17. What happens when scientists share their findings with others?

    _____

18. Where can you find information about safe experiments? _____

19. Why should you ask an adult to help you with your experiment?

    _____

20. Should you worry if you get different results? Why or why not?

    _____

FACTOID: It takes almost 250 Earth years for Pluto to complete one orbit around the sun.

PLACE STICKER HERE

Read the passage and answer the questions that follow.

Ava, Scientist

Ava had spent every spare moment of the last week working on her science fair project. She aspired to be a scientist one day. It was all she had ever wanted to do. Ava had her mind set on winning first prize. She could think of dozens of ways to use a new, powerful microscope. Her project wasn't going the way she had planned it, though. She pulled the lever, and several metal cans toppled to the floor. Ava stomped her foot with **exasperation**.

"Ava?" said Dad, tapping at her door. "How's it coming? Do you need any help?"

Ava sighed. "Nope, I just have to keep working until I get it right."

1. How would you describe Ava's character? Use details from the story to support your answer._____

_____

2. What does *exasperation* mean? What clues in the story helped you determine the meaning?_____

3. Write a brief summary of the story._____

_____

4. Rewrite part of the story using first-person point of view. Be sure to include details that might not be obvious from the third-person point of view._____

_____

_____

_____

_____

DAY 19

Look at the examples of parallel and perpendicular lines. Next to each shape, write how many pairs of parallel sides it has. Then, write how many pairs of perpendicular sides it has. (Your answer may sometimes be 0.)

Parallel Lines   Perpendicular Lines

5.   pairs of parallel sides _____

          pairs of perpendicular sides _____

6.   pairs of parallel sides _____

          pairs of perpendicular sides _____

7.   pairs of parallel sides _____

          pairs of perpendicular sides _____

8.   pairs of parallel sides _____

          pairs of perpendicular sides _____

9.   pairs of parallel sides _____

          pairs of perpendicular sides _____

Read the passage. Then, follow the directions.

In France, pancakes are called *crepes*. They are made with flour, eggs, and other ingredients. They are usually rolled up with different kinds of food inside. Most often, they are filled with fruit. In Mexico, pancakes made with cornmeal are called *tortillas*. Tortillas are filled with a mixture of foods. Tortillas can also be folded to make tacos.

On another sheet of paper, write a recipe for your favorite pancakes. Describe what you like to have on top of them.

PLACE STICKER HERE

Subtract to find each difference. Regroup if needed.

1. 5,042 −1,624	2. 2,710 −1,624	3. 4,200 −1,122	4. 7,106 −2,410	5. 3,340 −1,112
6. 9,824 −1,224	7. 6,831 −4,560	8. 7,605 −1,282	9. 6,351 −5,675	10. 8,001 −2,381

Round each number to the nearest place shown in parentheses ( ).

11. (ten thousand) 54,220 _____

12. (thousand) 3,728 _____

13. (thousand) 8,922 _____

14. (ten thousand) 46,003 _____

15. (hundred) 614 _____

16. (ten thousand) 18,138 _____

17. (hundred thousand) 198,425 _____

18. (ten thousand) 72,311 _____

CHARACTER CHECK: What is the hardest task that you have ever done? How did you feel when it was over? On a separate sheet of paper, write a paragraph about your experience.

Read the passage. Then, answer the questions.

Flags

A flag tells something special about a country or a group. For example, the United States flag has 13 red and white stripes for the country's first 13 colonies. It has 50 white stars on a blue background to represent the current 50 states. The Canadian flag has a red maple leaf on a white background between two bands of red. The maple tree is the national tree of Canada. Canadian provinces and U.S. states also have their own flags. The state flag of Texas has a large white star on a blue background on the left and two bands of red and white on the right. The star symbolizes Texas's independence from Mexico. Because of the flag's single star, Texas is called the *Lone Star State*. The flag of the Canadian province New Brunswick has a gold lion on a red background above a sailing ship. The lion stands for ties to Brunswick, Germany, and to the British king. The ship represents the shipping industry.

19. What is the main idea of this passage?
    A. A flag tells something special about the country or the group it represents.
    B. Some flags have maple leaves or lions on them.
    C. Many flags are red, white, or blue.

20. What does the United States flag look like? _____

    _____

    _____

21. What does the Canadian flag look like? _____

    _____

    _____

22. Why is Texas called the *Lone Star State?* _____

    _____

    _____

PLACE STICKER HERE

Spoon Bell

How can the pitch of sound be changed?

Pitch is a property of sound. A sound's pitch is determined by the frequency of the waves that are producing it. Pitch is often described in terms of the highness or lowness of a sound.

Materials:
- 30 inches (76 cm) of string
- metal spoon
- table

Procedure:
Tie the handle of the spoon to the center of the string. Wrap the ends of the string around your index fingers.

Place the tip of each index finger in each ear. Lean over so that the spoon hangs freely. Tap the spoon against the side of a table. Listen carefully. Then, record your observations on the chart below.

Shorten the string by wrapping more of it around your fingers. Tap the spoon against the table again. Then, record your observations on the chart below.

Trial	Observations
1	
2	

Which trial was louder? _____

What's This All About?
The vibrating molecules in the spoon hit the string's molecules. The energy is transferred up the string to your ears. When the vibrations travel across a long string, they spread out and have a lower frequency and a lower pitch. When you shorten the string, the movements are more compressed. This results in a higher frequency and a higher pitch.

BONUS

Germination

What conditions affect seeds as they germinate?

Materials:
- 2 small, empty jars
- masking tape
- pencil
- scissors
- 10 radish seeds
- sheet of paper towel
- permanent marker
- water

Procedure:

Open one jar. Draw four circles on the paper towel, using the mouth of the jar as your guide. Cut out the circles.

Put one paper towel circle in the bottom of each jar. Then, put five radish seeds into each jar. Put another paper towel circle over the radish seeds in each jar. Each jar should now have a "sandwich" made of two paper towel circles and five radish seeds.

Add enough water to each jar to moisten, but not drown, the paper towel circles. If you add too much water, pour it out; the seeds will be OK. Label your jars with the pencil and the masking tape. Label one jar *warm* and the other *cold*.

Put the *cold* jar in the refrigerator. Put the *warm* jar in a warm, dark place where it will not be disturbed, such as a drawer. Check the seeds every day for four days. Record your observations on a separate sheet of paper.

In which location did the seeds germinate faster? Why do you think this is?

_____

_____

What's This All About?

Several factors affect the germination of seeds. Mainly, seeds are affected by the amount of water available and the temperature. A seed waits until ideal weather conditions exist before sprouting. Some seeds must go through a period of dormancy, or sleep, and endure severe cold before they will germinate. You can put those seeds in a freezer for six weeks so that it feels like winter to them. They will then germinate when planted.

Product Map

A *product map* uses symbols to show which products are produced in certain places. Below is a product map of Wisconsin. Study the map. Then, answer the questions.

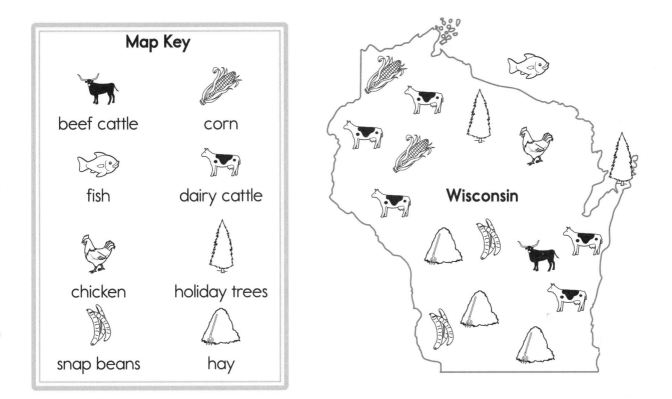

Map Key

beef cattle   corn

fish   dairy cattle

chicken   holiday trees

snap beans   hay

Wisconsin

1. What product does Wisconsin produce the most of? _____

2. Are more chickens or dairy cattle raised in Wisconsin? _____

3. Which two products are produced the least? _____

4. Judging from the map, does Wisconsin produce more livestock or crops?

   _____

5. Why might it be helpful to know where products are produced? _____

   _____

   _____

BONUS

Making a Map

Use an atlas to make a map of Africa. Draw and label the features in the list. Then, follow the directions.

Ahaggar Mountains
Atlas Mountains
Congo River
Lake Chad
Madagascar (Island)

Lake Tanganyika
Lake Victoria
Namib Desert
Nile River

Mediterranean Sea
Red Sea
Sahara Desert
Strait of Gibraltar

1. Color the deserts orange.

2. Draw brown triangles for the mountains.

3. Draw blue lines and circles for the rivers and lakes.

4. Draw a green line on the equator.

5. Draw red circles on the Tropic of Cancer and the Tropic of Capricorn.

Hemispheres

The prime meridian (0° longitude) and the meridian at 180° longitude divide Earth into two halves called the *eastern hemisphere* and the *western hemisphere*. Study the map below. Then, circle the correct hemisphere in parentheses to complete each sentence. Use an atlas or a world map if needed to help you identify each continent.

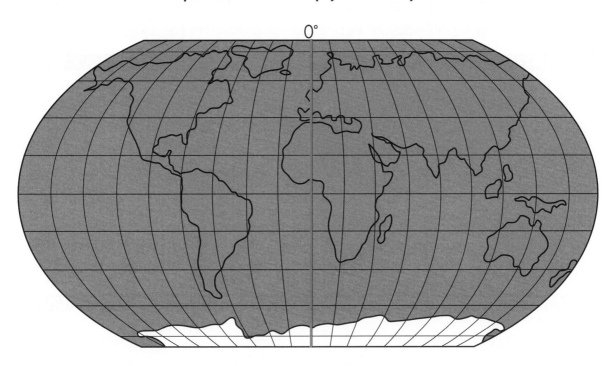

1. North America is in the (eastern, western) hemisphere.

2. Asia is mostly in the (eastern, western) hemisphere.

3. Africa is mostly in the (eastern, western) hemisphere.

4. South America is in the (eastern, western) hemisphere.

5. Europe is mostly in the (eastern, western) hemisphere.

6. Australia is in the (eastern, western) hemisphere.

BONUS

Take It Outside!

Take a notebook, a pencil, and a ruler outside. With an adult, find a garden or outdoor container garden where something is growing in groups, such as flowers, leaves, or vegetables. Locate the largest and smallest sample of each object and estimate their dimensions. Then, measure and compare each object. Continue estimating, measuring, and comparing objects until you are very close at estimating the exact answers.

You do not need a high-powered telescope to glimpse incredible sights in the night sky. With an adult, research the summer night sky to learn what stars can be seen where you live. Then, on a clear night, go outside with an adult. If you watch regularly, you might be able to see a meteor shower, a special star, or a distinctive constellation. Whatever the summer sky offers, keep a journal of your observations. If you do see a memorable constellation, make a sketch of it. Then, see if you can write a story or myth to go along with it. Try to find constellation myths at the library. How are they similar to and different from yours?

Archaeologists find and uncover objects. Then, they piece clues together to learn about the past. With your gardening gloves and a small shovel, go to an outdoor location where you have permission to dig. Dig several inches in a few different locations and examine what you find. Whether it is a quarter from 1978, an old button, or a fossil, you may be surprised by an interesting find. As you uncover the various items, consider how each object found its way into the earth. When you are finished, be sure to fill the holes you dug and clean up any mess that you made. Look at the items you found while digging. Do they have stories behind them? Write a short narrative in which you imagine the history of one of the items. Be sure to include descriptive details in your writing.

* See page ii.

Section I

Day 1/Page 3: 1. 324 apples; 2. 5 students; 3. $7.95; 4. $25.25; 5.–13. Answers will vary.; 14. B; 15. when snow hardens into ice over a long period of time; 16. A; 17. Antarctica and Greenland; 18. a lot of snow in winter and cool summers; 19. Glaciers can cause flooding where people live. Falling ice from glaciers may block mountain paths and roads. Icebergs that break off from glaciers may be a problem for ships at sea.

Day 2/Page 5: 1. play; 2. interest; 3. write; 4. cover; 5. spoon; 6. quick; 7. happy; 8. doubt; 9. kind; 10. cover; 11.–15.

15. SUMMER IS FUN; 16. 3 x 6 = 18; 6 x 3 = 18; 18 ÷ 6 = 3; 18 ÷ 3 = 6; 17. 9 x 4 = 36; 4 x 9 = 36; 36 ÷ 9 = 4; 36 ÷ 4 = 9; 18. 6 x 8 = 48, 8 x 6 = 48, 48 ÷ 6 = 8, 48 ÷ 8 = 6; 19. Eat, Fried, Worms; 20. Let, It; 21. Fair; 22. Piney, Woods; 23. How, Train, Your, Dragon; 24. Woods, Snowy, Evening; 25. Spaghetti; 26. Frozen

Day 3/Page 7: 1. 702; 2. 176; 3. 570; 4. 933; 5. 831; 6. 123; 7. 590; 8. 580; 9. 401; 10. 702; 11. Margot's mitten; 12. boys' towels; 13. Salim's bike; 14. birds' chirping; 15. Charles's hat; 16. maple tree's leaves; 17. Kylie's books; 18. Mariko's goggles; 19. dis-; 20. re-; 21. dis-; 22. un-; 23. in-; 24. in-; 25. dis-; 26. dis-; 27. 270; 28. 250; 29. 240; 30. 630; 31. 240; 32. 160

Day 4/Page 9: 1. 18 books; 2. 40 photos; 3. 42 birds; 4. 4 mini muffins; 5. are; 6. make; 7. her; 8. brings; 9. we; 10. see; 11.

their; 12. try; 13. 750 tires; 14. 2,250 tires; 15. large; 16. dried; 17. four; 18. good; 19. six; 20. many

Day 5/Page 11: 1. B; 2. 776 BC, Greece; 3. wreaths of olive branches; 4. The International Olympic Committee decided that the summer and winter Olympic Games should be held in different years.; 5. standing for or being an example of; 6. Host countries get a chance to show their culture to athletes, visitors, and spectators.; 7. 12; 8. 16; 9. 8; 10. 14; 11. 9; 12. 8; 13. 3; 14. 20; 15. softer, softest; 16. larger, largest; 17. flatter, flattest 18. sweeter, sweetest; 19. wider, widest; 20. cooler, coolest

Day 6/Page 13: 1. 5; 2. 64; 3. 9; 4. 7; 5. 6; 6. 18; 7. 99; 8. 84; 9. 13; 10. 66; 11. 6; 12. 30; 13. 2; 14. 30; 15. 49; 16. 32 cups; 17. $1,800; 18. 20 pounds; 19. 435 containers; The following words should be circled: elephant, tent, Mr. Chip, team, book, California, guitar, Lake Street, Kent, strength, engine, broccoli.; The following words should be underlined: sang, ate, fixed, laugh, landed, cleaned, yell, played, visited, write, see, tasted.

Day 7/Page 15: 1. respect; 2. generosity; 3. patience; 4. satisfaction; 5. silliness; 6. courage; 7. 30 students; 8. There are 95 students in 3rd grade. There are 100 students in 4th grade.; 9. social studies and math; 10. 20 more students like math better than reading in 3rd grade. 25 more students like math better than reading in 4th grade.; 11. 90; 12. 10; 13. 40; 14. 30; 15. 90; 16. 80; 17. 20; 18. 800; 19. 800; 20. 200; 21. 600; 22. CX, Before; 23. S; 24. CX, Unless; 25. C, and, but; 26. C, or; 27. CX, Although; 28. C, and; 29. CX, Because

Day 8/Page 17:

"I'd like to ride the Ferris wheel first," said Anya.; 2. "I'll meet you over there," said Kahlil, "after I get something to drink.";
3. "The fair seems even more crowded this year than last," commented Riley.; 4. "My favorite attraction is the bumper

cars," said Jacob, "but I also love the giant slides."; 5. "I can't go on anything that spins," said Kahlil, "because it makes me feel sick."; 6. Riley pointed and said, "There's the frozen lemonade stand."; 7. Anya asked, "What time are you meeting your parents?"; 8. "The line is too long for the rocket ship ride," decided Oliver.; 9. 5 x 3 = 15; 10. 7 x 4 = 28; 11. 5 x 1 = 5; 12. 2 x 3 = 6; 13. A; 14. A; 15. B; 16. 340 grams; 17. 10 kilograms; 18. 925 milliliters

Day 9/Page 19: 1. 140 yd.; 2. 10 in.; 3. 20 cm; 4. 43 in.; 5. Side A = 80 mm, Side B = 80 mm; 6. Side A = 5 cm, Side B = 5 cm; 7. 117 sq. ft.; 8. 51 sq. ft.; 9. 96 sq. in.; 10. 12 sq. ft.; 11. C; 12. to help rescue her family and help other slaves; 13. the network of people who helped slaves escape to freedom; 14. helped move slaves to freedom; 15. struggle between northern and southern states, mainly over slavery

Day 10/Page 21: $\frac{3}{6}$, $\frac{1}{2}$; $\frac{2}{3}$, $\frac{4}{6}$; $\frac{3}{3}$, 1; $\frac{1}{4}$, $\frac{2}{8}$; 1. My dog is ready to play, but my cat wants to nap.; 2. It may rain tonight, so the party will be indoors.; 3. A, B, D; 4. D; 5. A, B, C, D; 6. D; 7. A, B, C, D; 8. D; 9.–13. Sentences will vary.

Day 11/Page 23: 1. numb; 2. knead; 3. certain; 4. purchase; 5. sense; 6. wheat; 7. guide; 8. praise; 9. 6; 10. 6; 11. 7; 12. 9; 13. 4; 14. 8; 15. 6; 16. 4; 17. 5; 18. 3; 19.–22. Adjectives will vary.; 23. This or That; 24. This or That; 25. This or That; 26. These or Those

Day 12/Page 25: 1. 3; 2. 8; 3. 2; 4. My mom and stepdad were married in Portland, Oregon, on May 1, 1999.; 5. We had chicken, potatoes, corn, gravy, and ice cream for dinner.; 6. George Washington became the first U.S. president on April 30, 1789.; 7. Sam was born on June 16, 1947, in Rome, Italy.; 8. We saw deer, bears, elk, and goats on our trip.; 9. On July 24, 1962, in Boise, Idaho, I won the big race.; 10. 15, 3 x 5 = 15, 15 ÷ 3 = 5, 15 ÷ 5 = 3; 11. 7, 21 ÷ 7 = 3, 3 x 7 = 21, 7 x 3 = 21; 12. 5, 30 ÷ 5 = 6, 5 x 6 = 30, 6 x 5 = 30; 13. Rocky River, OH 44116; 14. Baltimore, MD 21218; 15. Harrisburg, PA 17111; 16. Lincoln, NE 68516; 17. Portland, OR

97215; 18. Colton, CA 92324

Day 13/Page 27: 1. 10, 5, 135; 2. 3, 3, 108; 3. 6, 6, 240; 4. 4, 4, 112; 5. 11, 11, 176; 6. knock; 7. hopped; 8. night; 9. baby; 10. different; 11. A; 12. Puerto Rico; 13. Pittsburgh; 14. helped people in Puerto Rico; 15. an earthquake; 16. to deliver supplies

Day 14/Page 29: 1. >; 2. <; 3. <; 4. >; 5. >; 6. <; 7. >; 8. >; 9. have good luck; 10. ill; 11. stay together; 12. ability to grow things; 13. cost a lot; 14.–19. Students should divide shapes as directed.; 20. 11:20; 21. 3:47; 22. 6:04; 23. 12:40; 24. 8:55; 25. 2:28

Day 15/Page 31: 1. 71°, 86 – 9 = 77, 77 – 6 = 71; 2. 1 inch, 4 × 12 = 48, 48 + 4 = 52, 53 – 52 = 1; 3. 6 muffins, 17 + 19 = 36, 42 – 36 = 6; 4. 50 miles, 10:00 to 3:00 = 5 hours, 5 × 10 = 50; 5. jazz, They are instruments.; 6. tire, They are tools.; 7. dog, They are birds.; 8. Moon, They are planets.; 9. peach, They are vegetables.; 10. lazy, They are flowers.;

15. will cook; 16. will visit; 17. will go; 18. will read; 19. will show

Day 16/Page 33: 1.–11. Answers will vary but may include: 1. saddest; 2. action; 3. direction; 4. safest/safety; 5. dirtiest; 6. hungriest; 7. invention; 8. preparation; 9. happiest; 10. heaviest; 11. honesty; 12. her; 13. him; 14. me; 15. us; 16. We; 17. They; 18. They, them; 19. well; 20. well; 21. better; 22. better; 23. best; 24. well; 25. worse

Day 17/Page 35: 1.–4. Answers will vary.; 5. -est, sad; 6. -est, hungry; 7. -tion, prepare; 8. -tion, invent; 9. -ty, taste; 10. -ty, certain; 11. -ty, loyal; 12. -tion, direct; 13. -tion, suggest; 14. -est, lovely; 15. -est, sure; 16. B; 17. the main character of the Anne of Green Gables series; 18. She lived with her grandparents and went to school in a one-room schoolhouse.; 19. when she was 17; 20. It was a best-seller. Two films and at least seven TV shows have been made from it.; 21. to see where Anne

Shirley grew up

Day 18/Page 37: 1. 80; 2. 90; 3. 84; 4. 96; 5. 78; 6. 94; 7. 76; 8. 95; 9. 76; 10. 84; 11. hatched; 12. looked; 13. used; 14. breathed; 15. changed; 16. started; 17. flattened; 18. vanished; 19. disappeared; 20. hopped; 21.–23. Answers will vary.; 24. / (slash) or dot; 25. good; 26. better; 27. best; 28. bad; 29. worst; 30. good

Day 19/Page 39: 1. C; 2. The ropes sometimes broke.; 3. pull the elevator back up if the cables broke; 4. 1853, New York Crystal Palace Exhibition; 5. the Eiffel Tower and the Empire State Building; 6. They continued to sell Otis's design.; 7. 63; 8. 24; 9. 40; 10. 18; 11. 15; 12. 64; 13. 54; 14. 21; 15. 20; 16. 49; 17. 48; 18. 16; Answers will vary.

Day 20/Page 41: 1. 224; 2. 155; 3. 190; 4. 188; 5. 125; 6. 148; 7. 207; 8. 161; 9. 166; 10. 154; 11. L; 12. A; 13. L; 14. L; 15. A; 16. A; 17. A; 18. A; 19. A; 20. A; 21. L; 22. L; 23. A; 24. L; 25. 42; 26. 31; 27. 34; 28. 31; 29. 10; 30. 11; 31. 23; 32. 11; 33. 12; 34. 10; 35. 14; 36. 20; 37. P, F, PR; 38. PR, F, P; 39. F, PR, P; 40. F, P, PR

Bonus Page 43: 1. The water causes the ink to dissolve and travel along the coffee filter.; 2. The inks separated into different colors.; 3. Answers will vary.; 4. able to dissolve in water; 5. the Procedure

Bonus Page 44: 1. The higher the ramp, the faster the object traveled.; 2. Answers will vary.; 3. It rolls faster.; 4. It asks a question that will be answered by doing the experiment.; 5. It makes it easy for the experimenter to see the relationship between the height of the ramp and the speed of the car.

Bonus Page 45: 1. 0°; 2. W; 3. E; 4. Students should trace the prime meridian.

Bonus Page 46: 1. 500 km; 2. 175 km; 3. 550 km; 4. 900 km

Bonus Page 47: 1. E; 2. H; 3. F; 4. J; 5. C; 6. D; 7. G; 8. I; 9. B; 10. A

Section II

Day 1/Page 51: 1. H; 2. B; 3. A; 4. C; 5. E;

6. G; 7. D; 8. F; 9. B; 10. D; 11. A; 12. F; 13. G; 14. E; 15. C; 16. H; Answers will vary.; 17. "Where is the big beach ball?" asked Jeff.; 18. Ilene exclaimed, "That is a wonderful idea!"; 19. "Come and do your work," Grandma said, "or you can't go with us."; 20. "Yesterday," said Ella, "I saw a pretty robin in the tree by my window."; 21. "I will always take care of my pets," promised Theodore.; 22. Rachel said, "Maybe we should have practiced more."; 23. Dr. Jacobs asked, "How are you, Pat?" ; Students' writing will vary.

Day 2/Page 53: Students' writing will vary.; The following words should be written under *Common Nouns*: ocean, class, holiday, boat, beans.; The following words should be written under *Proper Nouns*: Monday, November, July, Rex, North Carolina.; 1. B; 2. C; 3. two; 4. cent; 5. to; 6. sent; 7. too; 8. scent

Day 3/Page 55: 1. re-, to move again; 2. un-, not usual; 3. re-, to make new again; 4. un-, not common; 5. re-, to tell again; 6. umbrella; 7. Juan; 8. Amira and Becca; 9. Rachel; 10. toy; 11. bus; 12. wonderful; 13. warm; 14. worried; 15. who; 16. where; 17. weigh; 18. want; 19. won't

Day 4/Page 57: 1. $\overrightarrow{AB}$; 2. $\overleftrightarrow{GH}$; 3. $\overline{LM}$; 4. $\overleftrightarrow{CD}$; 5. $\overrightarrow{UT}$; 6. $\overline{WX}$; Students' writing will vary.; 7. pears; 8. seem; 9. flour; 10. right; 11. won; 12. dough; 13. B; 14. A; 15. C; 16. C; 17. A

Day 5/Page 59: 1. 3:30; 2. 55 minutes; 3. 4:00; 4. 3:45; 5. 6, 6; 6. 3, 3; 7. 8, 8; 8. 4, 4; 9. 4, 4; 10. 4, 4; 11. Shapes in #8, #9, and #10 have the same number of sides and vertices.; 12. 13,011; 13. 1,410; 14. 166; 15. 1,350; 16. 239; 17. 180; 18. 1,305; 19. 12,077; 20. 24,672; 21. 8,696; 22.–29. Students should circle the words in orange: 24. usually go; 25. drive slowly; 26. often begins; 27. plays loudly; 28. cheers excitedly; 29. pass near; 30. decorated beautifully; 31. never see

Day 6/Page 61: 1. 8, 16, 12, 18, 14; 2. 21, 15, 6, 12, 24; 3. 40, 32, 16, 28, 24, 36; 4. 45, 10, 30, 25, 35, 20; 5. pictures; 6. market; 7. cottage; 8. quarter; 9. pennies; 10. circus; 11. bell; 12. curtains; 13. chatter; 14. 60; 15.

54; 16. 124; 17. 91; 18. 107; 19. 15; 20. 80; 21. 28; 22. read; 23. knew; 24. told; 25. said; 26. heard; 27. bought; 28. found; 29. ate; 30. built

Day 7/Page 63: 1. 28, 32, and 18; 2. 16, 22, and 72; 3. 71, 82, and 98; 4. 63, 25, and 61; 5. 100, 206, and 200; 6. 79, 20, and 90; 7. make; 8. rolled; 9. enjoyed; 10. helps or helped; 11. places; 12. painted; 13. give; 14. I rode down the hill on a bike.; 15. My mom and I planted a garden in our backyard.; 16. All of the animals braced themselves when the elephants sneezed.; 17. Cory pulled a wagon full of bottles.; 18. 50 square units; 19. 157 square units; 20. 116 square units; 21. 172 square units

Day 8/Page 65: 1. My family visits Spring Grove, Minnesota, every year in the summer.; 2. Dear Grandpa,; 3. Yours truly,; 4. On October 9, 2009, Carolyn saw the play.; 5. My aunt and uncle live in North Branch, New York.; 6. Dear Jon,; 7. January 1, 2010; 8. Paris, Texas, is located in the northeastern part of the state.; 9. 150 liters; 10. 1 liter; 11. 10 kilograms; 12. 100 grams; 13. 11 inches; 14. 15 centimeters; 15. 92; 16. 30; 17. 33; 18. 125; 19. 51; 20. 64; 21. 16; 22. 71; 23. 18; 24. 40; 25. 22; 26. 17

Day 9/Page 67: 1. 3; 2. 2; 3. 5; 4. 3; 5. 4; 6. 4; 7. 5; 8. 6; 9. correct; 10. correct; 11. careful; 12. correct; 13. garden; 14. babies; 15. correct; 16. correct; 17. movie; 18. correct; 19. He lets people borrow his skateboard, and he can be counted on.; 20. Yes, because she takes turns and is fair.; 21. Answers will vary but may include going to school, going to summer camp, going to the recreation center, skateboarding, and riding bikes.; 22. Answers will vary. ; 23. It means that someone is always helpful and dependable.

Day 10/Page 69: 1. 36 people; 2. 144 plates; 3. 28 times as old; 4. 128 water balloons; 5.–8. Answers will vary.; 9. 394; 10. 663; 11. 258; 12. 28; 13. 226; 14. 312; 15. 2,688; 16. 3,589; 17. 2,835; 18. 5,464; 19.–26. Students should circle the words in orange.; 19. Antonio **is** going to soccer practice tomorrow.; 20. The girls **were**

planning a sleepover for Friday.; 21. Samir **has** read that book at least three times.; 22. Mom and Dad **were** expecting you for dinner.; 23. Colin **has** used that same duffel bag for the last five years.; 24. Brandy **will** bring snacks to the game.; 25. Zara **is** joining the French club.; 26. Tonight, we **are** studying for the quiz at Annie's house.

Day 11/Page 71: 1. 14,485; 2. 17,723; 3. 2,074; 4. 15,908; 5. 7,658; 6. 1,244; 7. 18,621; 8. 19,739; 9. 15,878; 10. 22,319; 11. snowflakes, dancers; 12. highway, parking lot; 13. tornado, train; 14. excitement, electrical current; 15. fingers, icicles; 16. 1,847; 17. 4,280; 18. 9,999; 19. 7,068; 20. 855; 21. 6,804; 22. 5,432; 23. positive; 24. magnify; 25. follow; 26. urgent; 27. nurse; 28. twirl; 29. return; 30. worse

Day 12/Page 73: 1. 561, 500 + 60 + 1; 2. 486, 400 + 80 + 6; 3. 4,826, 4,000 + 800 + 20 + 6; 4. 2,121; 5. 3,211; 6. I; 7. E; 8. B; 9. C; 10. D; 11. A; 12. H; 13. F; 14. G; 15. give the sunglasses to the girl; 16. Answers will vary.; Last summer, we went camping in Colorado. We went hiking and swimming every day. One time, I actually saw a baby white-tailed deer with spots. We also took photos of a lot of pretty rocks, flowers, and leaves. We had a great time. I didn't want to leave.

Day 13/Page 75: 1. 95°, obtuse; 2. 70°, acute; 3. 110°, obtuse; 4. 90°, right; 5. 70°, 25°, 70° + 25° = 95°; 6. B; 7. Empty the package into a microwave-safe bowl.; 8. water, milk, oatmeal, microwave-safe bowl, spoon, measuring cup; 9. B; 10. <; 11. >; 12. <; 13. >; 14. <; 15. <; 16. <; 17. <; 18. >; 19. >; 20. <; 21. <

Day 14/Page 77:

$1\frac{1}{4}$ inches; 1.–8. Answers will vary. Possible answers: 1. behind the curtains; 2. under a shady tree; 3. to the garden; 4. up the mountain; 5. on the table; 6. by the window; 7. beside Ella; 8. across the yard; 9. page 16; 10. page 40; 11. page 57; 12. ≠; 13. =; 14. ≠; 15. =

Day 15/Page 79: 1. 5,280 × 2 =10,560 feet; 2. 78 × 9 = 702 pounds; 3. 4,800 ÷ 120 = 40 hours; 4. 2,542 – 1,268 = 1,274 feet; Students' writing will vary.; 5. B; 6. C; 7. A; 8.–13. Answers will vary.

Day 16/Page 81: The following words should have three lines drawn beneath the first letter: Jane Goodall, Hampstead, London, Jubilee, Goodall, Gombe Stream National Park, Cambridge, Jane Goodall, Fifi, David, United Nations Messenger of Peace.; 1. Penny's dog Coco likes to eat special snacks.; 2. Oliver Owl is teaching Owen Owl to fly.; Students' writing will vary.

Day 17/Page 83: 1. cm; 2. m; 3. cm, cm; 4. km; 5. km; 6. m; 7. m; 8. km; 9. =; 10. >; 11. <; 12. >; 13. >; 14. <; 15. <; 16. <; 17. >; 18. >; 19. =; 20. <; 21. 4 × 5 = 20 books; 22. 108 ÷ 3 = 36 T-shirts; 23. 162 ÷ 18 = 9 years; 24. 133 ÷ 7 = 19 times as many; 25. Brooke will stay and tell Ms. Havel what happened.; 26. Answers will vary.

Day 18/Page 85: 1. $\frac{7}{12}$; 2. $\frac{7}{8}$; 3. $\frac{2}{6}$; 4. $\frac{1}{10}$; 5. who; 6. who; 7. that; 8. which; 9. that; 10. that; 11. Answers will vary.; 12. Answers will vary.; 13. A; 14. S; 15. A; 16. S; 17. A; 18. A; 19. S; 20. A; 21. S; 22. A; 23. A; 24. S; Earth, plant, Plants, oxygen, sunlight, heat

Day 19/Page 87: 1. 112; 2. 112; 3. 21; 4. 52; 5. 18; 6. 55; 7. 36; 8. 91; 9. 72; 10. 168; 11. 128; 12. 110; 13. 566; 14. 54; 15. 570; 16. two; 17. read; 18. paws; 19. too; 20. too; 21. Red; 22. to; 23. $\frac{3}{3}$ or 1; 24. $\frac{9}{6}$ or $\frac{3}{2}$; 25. $\frac{2}{6}$ or $\frac{1}{3}$; 26. $\frac{4}{6}$ or $\frac{2}{3}$; 27. $\frac{4}{4}$ or 1; 28. $\frac{2}{2}$ or 1; 29. $\frac{8}{8}$ or 1; 30. $\frac{7}{5}$; 31. $\frac{6}{10}$ or $\frac{3}{5}$; The following words should be written under *Compound Words*: buttermilk, airplane, snowstorm, football, daylight.; The following words should be written under *Words with Prefixes or Suffixes*: selection, replanted, sleepless, peaceful, unpacked.

Day 20/Page 89: 1. A; 2. A lot of rain falls quickly and fills the streets faster than they can drain.; 3. It could be swept away.; 4. listen to radio or TV news reports; 5. The author supports the point by stating the facts that trying to drive or walk in high water is very dangerous and that tap water can be made unsafe for drinking.; 6. listen to news reports to find out when you can return home and when the water from your tap will be safe to drink; 7. $\frac{3}{4}$; 8. $\frac{5}{3}$; 9. $\frac{12}{12}$ or 1; 10. $\frac{30}{8}$; 11. weightless; 12. thoughtful; 13. appointment

Bonus Page 92: heterogeneous

Bonus Page 93: 1. O; 2. N; 3. S; 4. Students should trace the equator.

Bonus Page 94: 1. Calgary; 2. Denver; 3. Boston; 4. Charleston; 5. Montreal; 6. Salt Lake City; 7. San Francisco

Bonus Page 95: Drawings will vary.

Section III

Day 1/Page 99: 1. 312; 2. 1,617; 3. 2,436; 4. 2,142; 5. 7,332; 6. 2,592; 7. 414; 8. 2,035; 9. 1,798; 10. 3,450; 11. go shopping for new clothes; 12. Answers will vary.; 13. $2.50; 14. $0.05; 15. $0.20; 16. $3.58; 17. $10.65; 18. $0.45; 19. $6.05; 20. $15.00; 21. deceive; 22. accompany; 23. exercise; 24. sincerely; 25. particular; 26. patient; 27. friend; 28. beautiful; 29. instead; 30. because; 31. guard; 32. although

Day 2/Page 101: 1. A; 2. a drawing that shows how different living things are connected; 3. B; 4. by explaining how all living things are connected in an ecosystem's food web; 5. 10; 6. 24; 7. 2; 8. 4; 9. 2; 10. 20; 11. 4; 12. 12

Day 3/Page 103: Answers will vary, but students should include support for their opinions.; 1. O; 2. O; 3. F; 4. O; 5. F; 6. F; 7. F; 8. O; 9. O; 10. A; 11. radio station; 12. newsreels in movie theaters or articles in newspapers; 13. Answers will vary. Possible answer: Edward Murrow was an American journalist who became famous for reporting from London on the radio during WWII.; 14. He started interviewing important people.

Day 4/Page 105: 1. 1 × 12, 2 × 6, 3 × 4; 2. 1 × 24, 2 × 12, 3 × 8, 4 × 6; 3. 1 × 15, 3 × 5; 4. 1 ×

28, 2 × 14, 4 × 7; 5. 1 × 36, 2 × 18, 3 × 12, 4 × 9, 6 × 6; 6. 1 × 32, 2 × 16, 4 × 8; 7. equal to; 8. more than; 9. less than; 10. equal to; 11. less than; 12. equal to; 13. less than; 14. equal to; 15. F, I; 16. I, F; 17. I, F; 18. F, I; 19. 15, 18, 21, 27; 20. 30, 36, 42, 54, 60; 21. 28, 32, 36, 40, 48; 22. 21, 18, 15, 12, 6; 23. 92, 90, 88, 84, 82

Day 5/Page 107: 1. read the books about Mexico to her grandmother; 2. Answers will vary.; 3. $\frac{3}{10}$ or 0.3; 4. $\frac{9}{10}$ or 0.9; 5. $\frac{7}{10}$ or 0.7; 6. $\frac{1}{10}$ or 0.10; 7. $\frac{5}{10}$ or 0.5; 8. 0.3; 9. 1.7; 10. 3.5; 11. $1\frac{9}{10}$; 12. $\frac{8}{10}$; 13. $3\frac{4}{10}$; 14. six empty water bottles; 15. musty brown cardboard box; 16. small pink teacup; 17. cozy gray wool sweater; 18. three large yellow plastic trucks; 19. small fresh Greek salad; 20. brown poisonous snake

Day 6/Page 109: 1. group of people living together; 2. in the city; 3. in the country; 4. $\frac{1}{6}$; 5. $\frac{2}{10}$ or $\frac{1}{5}$; 6. $\frac{1}{4}$; 7. $3\frac{4}{10}$ or $3\frac{2}{5}$; 8. $5\frac{1}{10}$; 9. $4\frac{1}{15}$; 10.–13. Answers will vary. Possible answers follow. 10. During the Depression, a girl writes in her journal about her worries on the farm and the help neighbors offer.; 11. Elizabeth is a hard worker. She worries about her family and their farm. She is grateful when neighbors help out and hopeful about the future.; 12. Tasks are easier when people work together. 13. first-person point of view, We learn about what Elizabeth's life is like and what her thoughts are. The reader gets the inside point of view.

Day 7/Page 111: 1. 1,500; 2. 6; 3. 25; 4. 1,000; 5. 8,500; 6. $\frac{1}{2}$; 7. 3; 8. 15; 9.–16. Students should circle the phrases in blue.: 9. <u>The cold weather</u> **caused frost to cover the windows.**; 10. <u>The falling snowflakes</u> **made my cheeks wet and cold;** 11. **Snow stuck to my mittens** <u>because I</u> had made a snowman.; 12. **The snowman melted** <u>from the heat of the sun.</u>; 13. <u>I swam so long in the pool</u>

that I had to put on more sunscreen.; 14. Cayce missed the bus <u>because she overslept.</u>; 15. <u>Because Shay watched a scary movie on TV,</u> she could not fall asleep.; 16. <u>The lady was thirsty,</u> so she went to get a glass of water.; Answers will vary, but students should include descriptive details and dialogue in their writing.; 17. <; 18. <; 19. >; 20. <; 21. >; 22. >; 23. >; 24. <; 25. <; 26. =; 27. <; 28. <

Day 8/Page 113: 1. B; 2. It is easy to get from one point in a city to another.; 3. A; 4. after a fire destroyed most of London, England; 5. Philadelphia's streets are wide, organized, and easy to walk down, and London's streets are not.; 6.–9. Check students' work for symmetry.; 10. hard; 11. honk; 12. fingers; 13. round; 14. fly; 15. small; 16. pencil

Day 9/Page 115: 1. Greg, Kipley, José, and Kira; 2. Day 1; 3. 2; 4. Naomi; 5. five; 6. He is not a new student.; Students' writing will vary.; 7. no; 8. yes; 9. no; 10. yes; 11. no; 12. no; 13.–16. Answers will vary. Possible answers: 13. I will be eating lunch.; 14. I am working on *Summer Bridge Activities.*; 15. I was riding my bike to the pool.; 16. I will be eating spaghetti and meatballs.

Day 10/Page 117: 1.–4. Answers will vary. Possible answers follow. 1. He wants to thank the king for helping Silenus.; 2. Dionysus is wiser than the king. He realizes that changing everything to gold is a terrible idea.; 3. Be careful what you wish for, and don't be greedy. Fables also have morals.; 4. The king will ask Dionysus to reverse his wish.; 5. $\frac{34}{100}$; 6. $\frac{70}{100}$; 7. $\frac{82}{100}$; 8. $\frac{65}{100}$; 9. $\frac{95}{100}$; 10. $\frac{75}{100}$; 11. $\frac{70}{100}$; 12. $\frac{95}{100}$; 13. $\frac{90}{100}$; 14. $\frac{89}{100}$; 15. $\frac{56}{100}$; 16. $\frac{32}{100}$; Answers will vary, but students' writing should include a logical sequence of events.

Day 11/Page 119: 1. B; 2. A; 3. A; 4. $3.39; 5. $6.41; 6. $2.89; 7. $1.06; 8. $2.89; 9. $6.28; 10. $2.09; 11. $2.11; 12. $3.89; 13. $1.89; Students' writing will vary.

Day 12/Page 121: 1. 1,807 R1; 2. 85 R7;

3. 177 R6; 4. 107; 5. 251 R2; 6. 1,156; 7. 125 R3; 8. 1,271; 9. 74 R4; 10. 159; 11. 111 R1; 12. 250 R2; Students' writing will vary.; 13. B; 14. Answers will vary but may include: boxes and books.; 15. Answers will vary but may include: lemonade and orange juice.; 16. Answers will vary but may include: air and helium.; 17. ice, water, steam/vapor; 18. Solids have a certain shape that is difficult to change. Liquids take the shape of the container they are in. Gases fill the space they are in.

Day 13/Page 123: 1. 1; 2. 1; 3. $\frac{5}{7}$; 4. 1; 5. $\frac{2}{7}$; 6. $\frac{5}{6}$; 7. I; 8. ewe; 9. eye; 10. where; 11. you; 12. wear; 13. <u>spect</u>acles; 14. <u>geo</u>logy; 15. thermo<u>meter</u>; 16. <u>aqua</u>rium; 17. <u>ped</u>al; 18. <u>inter</u>rupt; 19. <u>tri</u>plets; 20. auto<u>graph</u>; Students' writing will vary.

Day 14/Page 125: 1. C; 2. You will have a better chance of being a healthy adult later.; 3. The author gives the reasons that good health now can help you with your homework and help you become a healthy adult later.; 4. fresh fruit; 5. go for a walk with your family; 6. Students' paragraphs will vary.; 7. $\frac{1}{4} + \frac{1}{4} + 1\frac{1}{4} = 1\frac{3}{4}$, $2 - 1\frac{3}{4} = \frac{1}{4}$ hour; 8. $\frac{1}{3} + \frac{2}{3} + \frac{1}{3} = 1\frac{1}{3}$ miles; 9. $\frac{5}{8} + \frac{1}{8} + \frac{3}{8} + 2 = 2\frac{9}{8} = 3\frac{1}{8}$ pounds; 10. $\frac{16}{16} - \frac{5}{16} - \frac{9}{16} = \frac{2}{16}$ or $\frac{1}{8}$ of the cloth; The following words should be circled: Ninth, Street, Hillside, Maine, March, Skateboards, More, Rock, Avenue, Detroit, Michigan, Whom, It, May, Concern, It, Please, Sincerely, Wesley, Diaz.

Day 15/Page 127: 1. 16,266; 2. 46,300; 3. 1,140; 4. 25,312; 5. 5,442; 6. 60,312; 7. 55,638; 8. 10,962; 9. Raven has a new backpack. It is green with many zippers.; 10. Katie borrowed my pencil. She plans to draw a map.; 11. Zoe is outside. She is on the swings.; 12. Zack is helping Dad. Elroy is helping Dad too.; 13. B; 14. snowflakes; 15. C; 16. when it lands on a rosy maiden's cheek

Day 16/Page 129: 1. Answers will vary but may include: a forest, in the woods.; 2. summer; 3. the wind blowing through the pine trees, the creek nearby, and the screech of a hawk; 4. Answers will vary.; Students' writing will vary.; 5. 375; 6. 1,306; 7. 1,213; 8. 1,031; 9. 3,913; 10. 9,235; 11. 8,390; 12. 7,258; 13. 10,237; 14. 4,355; 15. 1,369,000; 16. 502,100,007; 17. three hundred seventy-five million four hundred three thousand one hundred one; 18. eight hundred ninety-four million three hundred thirty-six thousand forty-five

Day 17/Page 131: 1. 0.59; 2. 1.64; 3. 0.89; 4. 3.08; 5. 4.49; 6. 4.89; 7. 1.81; 8. 0.37; 9. 3.89; 10. 3.26; 11. B; 12. shorter; 13. Answers will vary but may include: key points, main idea, names of characters.; 14. 0.15; 15. 0.7; 16. 0.58; 17. 0.09; 18. 0.6; 19. 0.6; 20. 0.81; 21. 0.32; 22. 0.05; 23. 0.5; 24. 0.55; 25. 0.3; 26. S; 27. F; 28. R; 29. F; 30. S

Day 18/Page 133: 1. globe; 2. encyclopedia; 3. dictionary; 4. encyclopedia; 5. globe; 6. globe; 7. encyclopedia; 8. dictionary; 9. dictionary; 10. As a bird of prey, the American kestrel eats insects, mice, lizards, and other birds.; 11. Birds of prey, such as hawks, have hooked beaks and feet with claws.; 12. Falcons are powerful fliers, and they can swoop from great heights.; 13. The American kestrel, the smallest North American falcon, is only 8 inches (20.3 cm) long.; 14. "Kim, let's look at this book about falcons."; 15. A; 16. the supplies they use and the results they find; 17. Everyone learns a little more.; 18. library; 19. to help you set up and make sure you are being safe; 20. No, because some of the greatest scientific discoveries were made by mistake.

Day 19/Page 135: 1.–4. Answers will vary. Possible answers shown. 1. Ava is intelligent, persistent, and a little stubborn. She is very interested in science and she doesn't give up. She won't accept help.; 2. frustration, annoyance; Her project isn't going as planned, and she stomps her foot.; 3. Ava, who hopes to be a scientist one day, is working on a science fair project. She has some trouble but keeps working at it.; 4. Answers will vary.; 5. 2, 4; 6. 0, 1; 7. 2, 0; 8. 1, 0; 9. 4, 0

Day 20/Page 137: 1. 3,418; 2. 1,086; 3. 3,078; 4. 4,696; 5. 2,228; 6. 8,600; 7. 2,271; 8. 6,323; 9. 676; 10. 5,620; 11. 50,000; 12. 4,000; 13. 9,000; 14. 50,000; 15. 600; 16. 20,000; 17. 200,000; 18. 70,000; 19. A; 20. It has 13 red and white stripes and 50 white stars on a blue field.; 21. It has a red maple leaf on a white background between two bands of red.; 22. There is a single star on the state flag that symbolizes Texas's independence from Mexico.

Bonus Page 139: The second trial was louder.

Bonus Page 140: the warm jar; Answers will vary.

Bonus Page 141: 1. dairy cattle; 2. dairy cattle; 3. Students should list two of the three: fish, chicken, or beef cattle; 4. crops; 5. Answers will vary.

Bonus Page 142: Check students' drawings against an atlas for accuracy.

Bonus Page 143: 1. western; 2. eastern; 3. eastern; 4. western; 5. eastern; 6. eastern

weather

© Carson Dellosa

their

© Carson Dellosa

wood

© Carson Dellosa

night

©© Carson Dellosa

whose

© Carson Dellosa

shown

© Carson Dellosa

write

© Carson Dellosa

threw

© Carson Dellosa

our

© Carson Dellosa

would

they're

whether

shone

who's

knight

are

through

right

borrow
(antonym)

© Carson Dellosa

wide
(antonym)

© Carson Dellosa

succeed
(antonym)

© Carson Dellosa

dependable
(synonym)

©© Carson Dellosa

annoy
(synonym)

© Carson Dellosa

strange
(synonym)

© Carson Dellosa

Graceful is to
clumsy as hot is to:

© Carson Dellosa

Pillows are to soft
as boards are to:

© Carson Dellosa

Fish is to swim
as birds are to:

© Carson Dellosa

fail (antonym)	narrow (antonym)	lend (antonym)
© Carson Dellosa	© Carson Dellosa	© Carson Dellosa
unusual (synonym)	irritate (synonym)	reliable (synonym)
© Carson Dellosa	© Carson Dellosa	© Carson Dellosa
fly	hard	cold
© Carson Dellosa	© Carson Dellosa	© Carson Dellosa

audi
(hear or listen)

dict
(speak)

port
(carry)

vis
(see)

auto
(self)

bio
(life)

graph
(write or draw)

ology
(study)

scope
(see, watch)

transport
export
portable

predict
dictator
contradict

audience
auditorium
audition

biography
biologist
antibiotic

automatic
autograph
automobile

vision
supervisor
invisible

microscope
telescope
stethoscope

biology
zoology
geology

autograph
paragraph
photograph

acute angle	right angle	point
© Carson Dellosa	© Carson Dellosa	© Carson Dellosa
obtuse angle	line	line segment
©© Carson Dellosa	© Carson Dellosa	© Carson Dellosa
parallel lines	perpendicular lines	ray
© Carson Dellosa	© Carson Dellosa	© Carson Dellosa

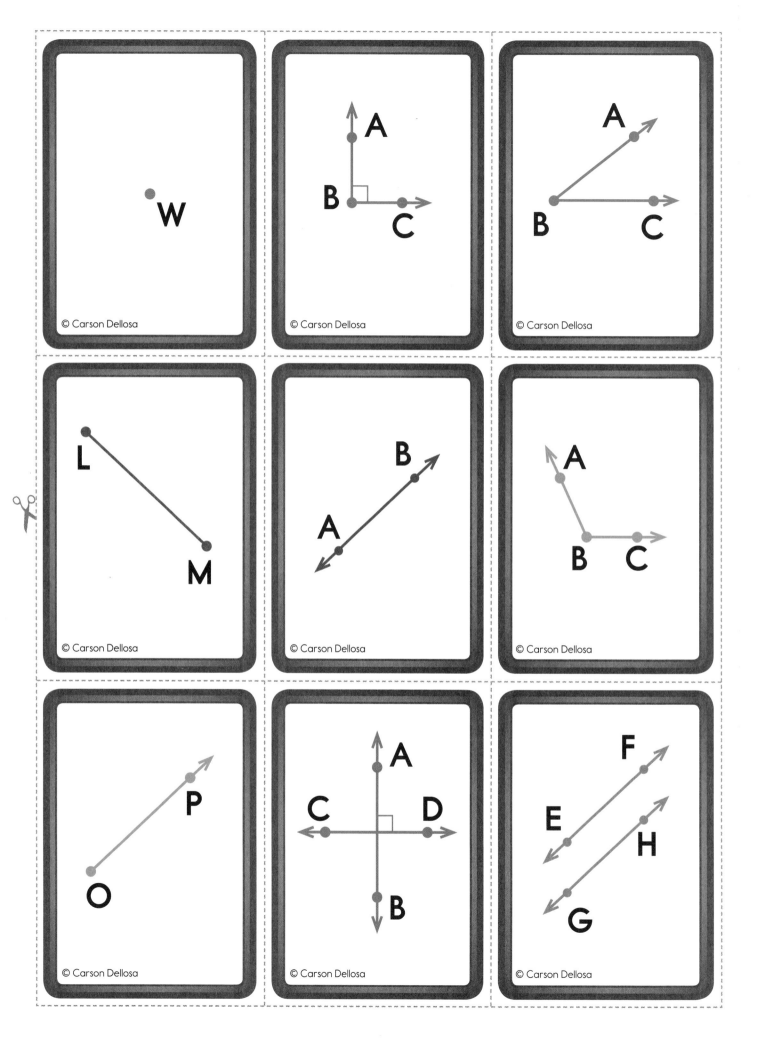

2,485

© Carson Dellosa

639

© Carson Dellosa

49,561

© Carson Dellosa

2,749

©© Carson Dellosa

98

© Carson Dellosa

217

© Carson Dellosa

326,513

© Carson Dellosa

3,746

© Carson Dellosa

493

© Carson Dellosa

40,000 + 9,000
+ 500 + 60 + 1

© Carson Dellosa

600 + 30 + 9

© Carson Dellosa

2,000 + 400
+ 80 + 5

© Carson Dellosa

200 + 10 + 7

© Carson Dellosa

90 + 8

© Carson Dellosa

2,000 + 700
+ 40 + 9

© Carson Dellosa

400 + 90 + 3

© Carson Dellosa

3,000 + 700
+ 40 + 6

© Carson Dellosa

300,000 + 20,000
+ 6,000 + 500
+ 10 + 3

© Carson Dellosa

Factor pairs of 12

© Carson Dellosa

Factor pairs of 18

© Carson Dellosa

Factor pairs of 20

© Carson Dellosa

Factor pairs of 24

©© Carson Dellosa

Factor pairs of 32

© Carson Dellosa

Factor pairs of 36

© Carson Dellosa

Factor pairs of 48

© Carson Dellosa

Factor pairs of 56

© Carson Dellosa

Factor pairs of 60

© Carson Dellosa

1 x 12
2 x 6
3 x 4
© Carson Dellosa

1 x 18
2 x 9
3 x 6
© Carson Dellosa

1 x 20
2 x 10
4 x 5
© Carson Dellosa

1 x 24
2 x 12
3 x 8
4 x 6
© Carson Dellosa

1 x 32
2 x 16
4 x 8
© Carson Dellosa

1 x 36
2 x 18
3 x 12   4 x 9
           6 x 6
© Carson Dellosa

1 x 48
2 x 24
3 x 16   4 x 12
           6 x 8
© Carson Dellosa

1 x 56
2 x 28
4 x 14
7 x 8
© Carson Dellosa

1 x 60
2 x 30
3 x 20   4 x 15
           5 x 12
           6 x 10
© Carson Dellosa

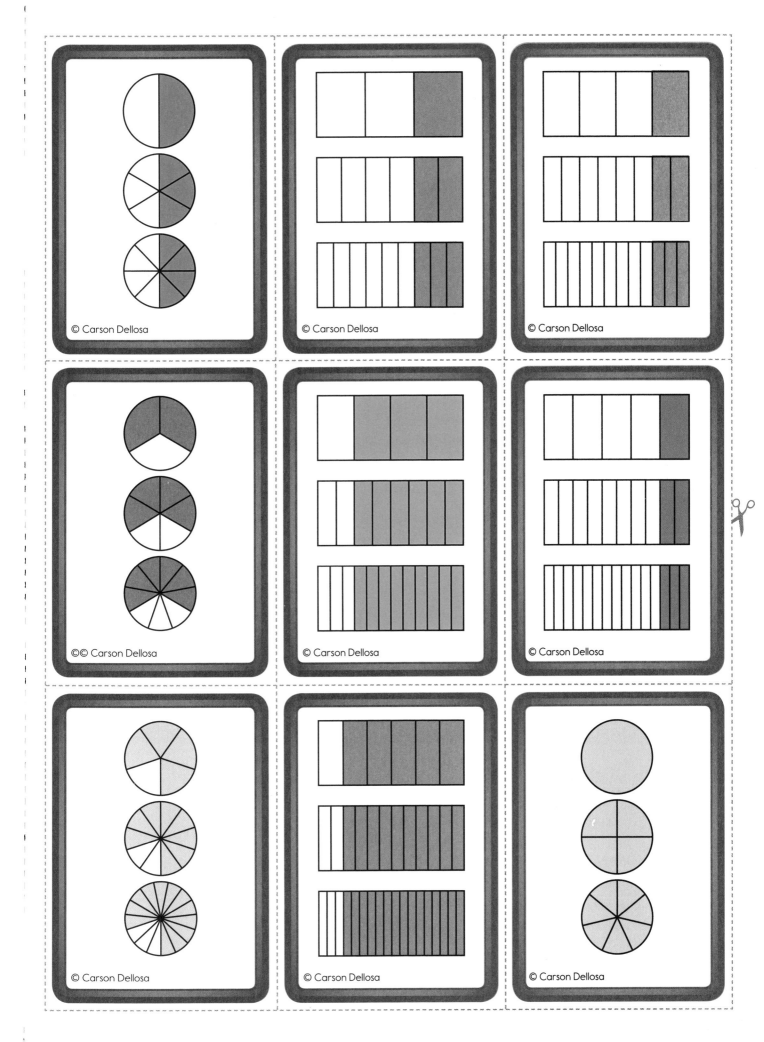

© Carson Dellosa

$$\frac{1}{4}$$

$$\frac{2}{8} = \frac{1}{4}$$

$$\frac{3}{12} = \frac{1}{4}$$

© Carson Dellosa

$$\frac{1}{3}$$

$$\frac{2}{6} = \frac{1}{3}$$

$$\frac{3}{9} = \frac{1}{3}$$

© Carson Dellosa

$$\frac{1}{2}$$

$$\frac{3}{6} = \frac{1}{2}$$

$$\frac{4}{8} = \frac{1}{2}$$

© Carson Dellosa

$$\frac{1}{5}$$

$$\frac{2}{10} = \frac{1}{5}$$

$$\frac{3}{15} = \frac{1}{5}$$

© Carson Dellosa

$$\frac{3}{4}$$

$$\frac{6}{8} = \frac{3}{4}$$

$$\frac{9}{12} = \frac{3}{4}$$

© Carson Dellosa

$$\frac{2}{3}$$

$$\frac{4}{6} = \frac{2}{3}$$

$$\frac{6}{9} = \frac{2}{3}$$

© Carson Dellosa

$$1$$

$$\frac{4}{4} = 1$$

$$\frac{7}{7} = 1$$

© Carson Dellosa

$$\frac{5}{6}$$

$$\frac{10}{12} = \frac{5}{6}$$

$$\frac{15}{18} = \frac{5}{6}$$

© Carson Dellosa

$$\frac{4}{5}$$

$$\frac{8}{10} = \frac{4}{5}$$

$$\frac{12}{15} = \frac{4}{5}$$

© Carson Dellosa

SummerBridge ACTIVITIES®

Congratulations!

This certifies that

_____

Name

has completed **Summer Bridge Activities.**

_____

Parent's Signature